It can be as intangible and fleeting as watching an iceberg crowded with basking seals slide by, or a deep and powerful childhood memory of spine-tingling excitement as a holiday destination is reached. Either way, the heart is touched. An indelible impression is made; that place, that moment, lives forever.

In this evocative, moving and entertaining collection, thirty prominent Australians reveal what sets some places apart for them. They describe the magic moments, vivid impressions, memorable sights or incidents that have created special places in their hearts.

Places in the Heart spans the globe and embraces several decades. Memories of golden childhoods; celebrations of special corners of Australia; love affairs with foreign fields, pilgrimages back to mother countries; and passion for unique cuisines results in a rich mix of anecdote, memoir, history, social comment and fun.

SUSAN KUROSAWA is an award-winning journalist and writer. She has been the travel editor of *The Australian* since 1992, and a columnist with its *Australian Magazine* for the past six years. In 1994 she was named Journalist of the Year by the Pacific Asia Travel Association. Susan's previous books are *The Joy of Travel*, *That's Life* and *Teenspeak: A Survival Guide for the Verbally Challenged Parent*. She also contributed to the anthologies *Hot Sand*, *Off the Rails* and *Cutting the Cord*. Her new book, *Coasting*, will be published by Hodder Headline in 1999.

Places in
the Heart

Thirty prominent Australians
reveal their special corners
of the world

edited and compiled by
SUSAN KUROSAWA

SCEPTRE

SCEPTRE

Published in Australia and New Zealand in 1997
by Hodder Headline Australia Pty Limited
(A member of the Hodder Headline Group)
10–16 South Street, Rydalmere NSW 2116

This paperback edition published in 1998

Published in association with Belladonna Books
39 Palmer Street, Balmain NSW 2041

**National Library of Australia
Cataloguing-in-Publication data**

Places in the heart: thirty prominent Australians reveal
their special corners of the world.

ISBN 0 7336 0956 2 (pbk.)

1. Travel—Guidebooks. 2.Travelers' writings. 3.
Voyages around the world. I. Kurosawa, Susan.

910.4

Jacket design by Beth McKinlay
Text design and typesetting by Bookhouse Digital, Sydney
Printed in Australia by Griffin Press, Adelaide

Jane Holmes: photograph by Andy Laidlaw
Glenn A. Baker: photograph by Mark Leonard
Marele Day: photograph by Galea McGregor
Susan Kurosawa: photograph by Michael Chetham
Tony Wheeler: photograph by Jon Krakauer
Sorrel Wilby: photograph courtesy of the Nine Network

To Graeme,
who holds a special place in my heart,
and in memory of
Shirley Peach and Gileen Dyer

Acknowledgments

With special thanks to Mary Rose Trainor,
my editorial coordinator, and her team of researchers:
Christine McCabe, Leonie Coombes, Nellie Blundell,
Anita Roberts and Robert Beattie.

Contents

Preface

S.K., Brighton Pier, England, 1956

How hard it is to escape from places. However carefully one goes they hold you—you leave bits of yourself fluttering on the fences, little rags and shreds of your very life.

Katherine Mansfield

Most of us form passionate emotional attachments during our lives. Not just to soul-mate partners and cherished children but to very special places which tug so firmly at our heartstrings that each time we venture there, we leave a little bit of ourselves behind. These places can be entire countries or simply cities, regions or landscapes. We may visit so often that we feel we could draw, from memory, detailed maps of their most intimate nooks and corners. Or our encounters may be rare and fleeting and yet, like an enchanting face glimpsed across a crowded room, the imprint is unforgettable. Other places appeal so much that we simply live there, rooted and flourishing like cared-for plants, waxing lyrical to all-comers about our special piece of the planet.

When we examine the notion of adopted place and heart, examples come to mind of very grand partnerships. Who can think of French Polynesia, for example, minus the vibrant paintings of Paul Gauguin, or consider Bali without Donald Friend? I can never read of the Greek Islands without imagining George Johnston and Charmian Clift in a little whitewashed house, penning gentle tales of village life, taking ouzo with lunch and snoozing in the lemon-scented afternoon.

Whenever the Arab world is mentioned, I have an instant vision of Gertrude Bell aboard a camel, swathed in veils, queen of her desert domain. Visit Western Samoa and the legend lives on of Robert Louis Stevenson, its adopted son, on whom the most honoured of titles, Tusitala, or 'teller of tales', was bestowed. Wanderers such as these took the concept of expatriatism to ultimate lengths—becoming indivisible from the chosen place itself.

Other travellers do not jump the divide to expatriate status but remain as distant admirers of places which have captured their hearts. The reality of a life to be lived elsewhere keeps them away from beloved countries or cities for long stretches of time. They realise, too, deep in their hearts, that what they suffer is a 'someplace else' syndrome—they long to be *there* but they also want to be safely at home. Such is the case with me and India.

Since I first set foot there, in Bombay, in the early 1980s, I have been caught between intense love and heart-pumping terror. On that initial drive from the airport, leprous hands came thrusting through the taxi window, I saw people sleeping in cardboard boxes by open sewers, and by the time I arrived at my hotel I was sobbing in disbelief. It took days before I could venture further than the cocoon of the lobby and confront not just off-the-scale poverty but my ability to deal with scenes too alien to have believed possible.

What keeps me returning is the need to know more about myself—a common thread curving through many of the interviews in *Places in the Heart,* and especially those in the very nostalgic sections dealing with rosy childhood memories and ancestral links.

In the first section, *Those Were the Days,* each contributor evokes a heartfelt and often amusing picture of holidays and experiences gone by. TV presenter Jeff Watson recalls bucket-and-spade adventures and a cast of characters at Mrs Evans's boarding house in the little seaside town of Tenby in South Wales. Playwright Barry Dickins reminisces about his suburban boyhood in Melbourne and the wondrous, wide-eyed drama of 'going to town' with his beloved grandmother, Gert.

Travel industry leader Sarina Bratton explains her love of the surfy Australian coast—especially Kingscliff, just south of the Queensland border with NSW, where her mother could blithely sweep the sand straight out of the family's little holiday cabin onto the beach. The Australian Brandenburg Orchestra's artistic director, Paul Dyer, describes family holidays at Ettalong on the NSW Central Coast—zinc-creamed noses, a salty tang to the breeze, and fish and chips for tea. Poet and author Kate Llewellyn's chosen topic is her childhood in Tumby Bay, South Australia, where the landscape is bleached of all colour and the sea is so pale and clear you can see your toenails in the water.

This is My Place is a wonderfully patriotic section in which six special Australians provide an insight into their favourite corner of the country. Media personality Bill Peach talks about the Upper Murray, the region of his forebears, and describes how every time he goes back, "I feel that tie of blood, the intrinsic bond so important to our Aboriginal people. It's where you know your ancestors are buried."

Photographer and publisher Steve Parish describes his affinity with the wildness of Kakadu and how his experiences there have taught him the wisdom of Aboriginal philosophy. Art entrepreneurs John and Ros Moriarty of Balaranji Design explain their connection with the remote Coorong in South Australia, where their weekender and studio sits "like a cradle", waiting to welcome them home.

Leading crime writer Marele Day uses Sydney as a backdrop for her popular Claudia Valentine books and she talks about her lasting love affair with the harbour and its water-facing reaches. "Sydney," she says, "is racy, trashy and hedonistic but I love every minute of it." Writer and commentator Richard Neville waxes lyrical about his bushland home in the "elemental" Blue Mountains west of Sydney: "You're close to primal forces . . . it's a turbulent place to live." Forget those old East Coast rivalries—Melbourne-born actor Graeme Blundell is crazy about Sydney's Kings Cross and recounts his experiences of living for close to 20 years on its sometimes dangerous fringe, "where you can walk three blocks without leaving the scene of the crime!"

As the name vividly suggests, the section called *Love at First Sight* is all about knee-jerk attraction: the contributors to this section have become instantly and irrecoverably infatuated by some of the most colourful corners of the globe. TV personality and former Test cricketer Mike Whitney tells how he was enveloped by India the minute he got off the plane—a theme that continues in my own accounts of adventures in the baffling subcontinent, including a stint as a movie-extra bar girl in Bollywood, India's answer to Tinsel Town. Honorary consul for Nepal and adventure travel company founder Christine Gee talks of trekking the Himalaya; on her first mountain-top morning, at Pokhara, she popped her head outside the tent and was transported by the scenery. "I felt I had left the earth," she says.

Journalist, historian and documentary filmmaker Tim Bowden enthuses about his fascination for Antarctica and how it keeps calling him back. "It could well be the silence," he explains, "for silence actually exists in Antarctica . . . an ABC sound recordist once succeeded in recording total silence out on the ice cap." Reporter and broadcaster Jane Holmes tells of her walks on the wild side in deepest Africa—including swimming with elephants at the unique Abu's Camp in Botswana.

Ancestral Ties is a section in which Australians return to their original homeland—or that of their families—and describe the process of discovering their roots. Award-winning documentary filmmaker Daizy Gedeon talks about the blossoming of her relationship with Lebanon and the overcoming of entrenched prejudice. Leading architect Harry

Seidler reveals his enduring ties with Vienna and remembers being sent to a strict school where a bad mark meant learning ten verses of Homer by heart—to be recited in front of the class. Comedian Vince Sorrenti recounts amusing escapades in Italy and describes a pilgrimage to the villages from which his parents migrated to Australia in the 1950s.

Travel industry doyenne Mary Rossi talks of a year spent living in Florence with Theo, her husband of Italian descent, and their large family. Upon arrival in Florence, Mary was charmed at first sight by the villa arranged for the Rossi clan by her dear friend, Fiamma Ferragamo. "Isn't it wonderful!" Mary exclaimed to Theo. It turned out to be the gatehouse.

Multi-award-winning chef Tetsuya Wakuda speaks of the complexities of his Japanese heritage and his love for his adopted city, Sydney. "My parents [in Japan] sometimes get upset about not seeing me and tell their friends they don't have a son any more . . . they do—it's just that he's an Aussie."

The Love of Food section deals with "galloping gourmet" travellers and their experiences around the globe. Melbourne chef and restaurateur Stephanie Alexander talks of the Perigord and Dordogne regions of south-west France, where the country markets are "enchanting" and "there's a sense that buying food is a life-enriching tradition".

Asian cookery expert Charmaine Solomon shares her wide knowledge of Asian markets and their often curious bounty, while admitting she is a hopeless haggler. "Whose side are you on, Charmaine?" her husband and co-shopper, Reuben, will often ask. TV presenter Pria Viswalingam recalls his childhood in Malaysia and the parade of food hawkers who would visit his street. "You'd hear a horn," he reminisces, "and it would be the Chinese guy with *char sui bao* . . . I'd buy a little collection and eat it myself. I even got to the point where I'd stash it . . . under a bush, go and have dinner and later go out and eat it by myself."

Francophile author Marion Halligan recalls the happiest of times with her family in Sévérac and offers insights into the notion of "a love affair" with a country, comparing such a relationship with that which exists between people. "It's very much a matter of chemistry," she concludes.

Finally, in *The Global Village*, contributors whose hearts belong to particular landscapes and pastimes describe their consuming passions. Author and adventurer Sorrel Wilby explains her love of remote and sometimes almost inaccessible places, especially in Africa and Nepal, while mountaineer Tim Macartney-Snape recounts his most memorable climbing adventures and discusses what spurs him on to the top—it's "a totally absorbing intellectual challenge", he concludes.

Eco-tourism operator Mimi Macpherson talks about her successful whale-watching operation at Queensland's Hervey Bay and reveals how the first time she heard a whale singing, over an underwater microphone, she was reduced to tears. Tony Wheeler, founder of the enormously successful Lonely Planet publishing house, is a committed walker and he describes his favourite trails in Europe and Asia and passes on tips for those fit enough to follow in his footsteps.

Another energetic inclusion in this section is pop-music guru and travel addict Glenn A. Baker, who tells zany tales of his myriad adventures in the world's most offbeat places, including Indonesia's Torajaland where the complicated and protracted funeral rituals are among the most bizarre on earth. "These people live for death," is Glenn's conclusion.

My sincere thanks to these compulsive, generous and often fearless travellers for sparing the time to speak of their places in the heart and for their willingness to share their very special insights and observations.

Susan Kurosawa
Sydney, 1997

Chapter 1

THOSE WERE THE DAYS

Memories of golden
childhood holidays

Oh, I do like to be beside the seaside

JEFF WATSON
TV presenter

"My first encounter with Tenby in South Wales was at the end of World War II when I was about seven years old. It was very difficult to take holidays in England at that time because many of the beaches on the south coast still had barbed wire, tank traps and landmines to keep the Nazis out. I recall on one of our English holidays we went to a beach which was littered with metal and pieces of planes and barbed wire and my brother picked up something which started ticking and my father snatched it off him and threw it out to sea. It didn't explode! But nobody had expected the Nazis in Wales, so the seaside was pretty safe.

It was an interminable drive to get there, an expedition of gargantuan proportions, because in those days there were no motorways. We lived in Birmingham where my father had an engineering factory and we drove down in our black Ford 8. The licence plate was DLR577 and it had a hole in the back floor! We were lucky to have a petrol allowance—there was still rationing. We would pile things on the roof. The boot would be partly open and tied with bits of string. The suitcases were cardboard and they'd be stuck out of the boot so if it rained, as it invariably did, all our belongings would end up damp.

We'd set out for around two weeks in the August school holidays and we used to take a very circuitous route to Tenby through the Brecon Beacons, which is a beautiful part of Wales. Although it was only 160 miles from Birmingham, it used to take about eight hours as during the war all the signposts had been turned around because the English were completely paranoid about Nazi paratroopers being dropped. So the first sign would say 'Brecon 6 miles' and the next

4

would say 'Brecon 10 miles' and the next sign would be pointing back to where you had come from. It was well into the 1950s before the proper signposts were in place again.

Finally, we'd arrive at Tenby. It's a very beautiful seaside resort, rather dignified, with a veneer of respectability and no fun pier or the razzmatazz of, say, Brighton or Blackpool. I've been back perhaps ten times in the past twenty years and it's still relatively unchanged. It has wide, sweeping beaches and, although memory tends to exaggerate everything, even the weather, it always seemed to be warm when I was a boy.

We used to stay at Mrs Evans's Boarding House in Upper Frog Street. There was a Lower Frog Street, too. Mrs Evans's was like something out of *Monty Python's Flying Circus*: 'Here's Mr and Mrs So-and-So from West Hartlepool. He's an engineer. You'll get on well with him!' There'd be the same guests year after year, sitting at the same tables in the gloomy dining room. Conversation was always kept to a low din and children would have to behave.

Mrs Evans's was about four storeys tall, a flat-fronted building right on the street. Like most English boarding houses, the bathrooms would be down the hall. We kids would be put in rooms at the top of the house and we'd try to slide down the banisters of the huge Victorian staircase. I can see Mrs Evans, even now—floral pinny, hair caught up in a scarf tied at the front, like a housewife out of *Coronation Street*.

The thing that really got up my nose was that my brother, Graham, and I were always put to bed after tea—good fish and chips, usually. Because of the summer twilight, it wouldn't be dark until about ten. The sun would stream through the skylight window and we would hear everyone enjoying themselves at the pub. There was no TV, of course.

We'd read in bed or talk about the films we'd seen. I used to cry at the *Lassie* ones and loved *Hopalong Cassidy* and *Tarzan*. Marvellous directors like the Boulting brothers were turning out very funny British films with lots of sight gags which appealed to the seaside holiday crowd who wanted a jolly good laugh.

The picture theatre—I think it was called the Empire, as they tended to be—was built of clapboard with 'loox-ury' leatherette seats. The projector would break down halfway through the film or it'd be out of focus or there'd be a hair in the gate but nobody complained. Everyone smoked. We'd eat Smiths crisps with little twists of paper containing salt; we'd fumble with the packet in the dark and get the salt everywhere. There was food rationing up to about 1954 or '55 so the only sweets available were the cheap, tooth-rotting variety. There was a rock shop: we'd buy pink and white striped candy sticks with the word Tenby running along. Then we'd bite right into the rock to see if the writing went all the way to the centre. We had fizzy pop to drink—sweet lemonade or orangeade. We'd shake the bottle up and this sticky foam would come out the top. There wasn't much fruit, just Valencia oranges. The Nazis had been torpedoing our boats coming from the West Indies so there was nothing like a banana. My father used to say, 'What do you call that yellow fruit which you have to peel?' Lots of English people of my vintage have terrible teeth from too many sugary seaside treats!

During the day, we'd watch the lifeboats being launched. Brave matelots would go thundering down the ramp and into the ocean to rescue seamen. My brother and I would collect as many sea creatures as we could—little fish, crabs and all sorts of things—and we'd take them back to Mrs Evans's in our metal buckets. Mine was green and it lasted for years. There was no plastic in those days. There are some interesting caves at Tenby and they go a long way under the town. Most of the boarding houses and hotels sit on very high rock overlooking the bay and there are passages and tunnels underneath. We'd climb into them at low tide and it was very exciting.

My mother would take me to Woolworth's. We'd discover I'd left something I needed behind in Birmingham so off we'd go to shop. Woolworth's was all crimson with gilt window frames. There were busty assistants in red tunics serving liquorice all-sorts. It was an extraordinary emporium—from a child's perspective, it contained every treasure you'd ever need. It's still there, opposite the church, but these days, it's all self-service and video games.

At the end of the holidays, when we headed back to Birmingham, which is about as far from the sea as you can get in England, I'd take buckets of sand and all the shells I'd collected. One year, I put seaweed, which I thought was rather exotic, in the boot and as it warmed up during the long trip home, there was this terrible smell. My father made me throw it out.

Dad was an amateur entomologist—he was into butterflies and moths. The hills around Tenby are covered with gorse and there was always a chance of spotting something rare. Once we saw a monarch—it's a species which has been known to cross the Atlantic from America; apparently they get up in the jetstream. It was fun identifying all the butterflies—the Lulworth skipper, the red admiral, the peacock and so on. My father loved fishing, too. He'd leave my brother and I behind on Goscar Rock to play in the rockpools and make sandcastles and he'd stand on the jetty fishing but usually he got nothing. One memorable afternoon, a shoal of mackerel came into the bay and he caught at least fifty. The story was exaggerated as the years passed—up to at least a hundred! There he was, catching fish after fish, but mackerel are practically inedible. He went to the pub to celebrate and arrived back at Mrs Evans's smelling of Guinness. My mother was very thin-lipped about it and he was in the doghouse for days.

The sand at Tenby is very much like the texture of Australian beaches. It's not pebbly like the English Riviera nor a miserable seafront like Bognor Regis where there are seagulls coughing in the mist. My swimming costume was like a girl's one-piece and covered my chest. It was scratchy and smelt of mothballs from being stored away during winter. I think my mother knitted it: she'd put horizontal stripes to make me look less emaciated. My parents never wore shorts, never exposed their legs even on the warmest days. My father had an outfit for the beach: an open-necked shirt and a jacket. If he took off his jacket, it was a heatwave. He had gabardine flannels with turn-ups—these big, flappy trousers—and of course he wore socks with his sandals. I never actually saw him knot a hankie in the corners and put it on his head but I think he might have, to amuse my mother. She wore a cotton print dress, with a belt. The sun was never strong enough for a hat.

I never really learned to swim properly until I arrived in Australia because the water in Britain is usually too cold, even in summer. We'd rent deckchairs for sixpence a day—sometimes we'd be cunning and we'd wait until other people vacated theirs and we'd run to claim them. My parents would stare moodily out to sea—just like British holidaymakers do today, as described so well by Paul Theroux in his book, *Kingdom by the Sea*. My mother would read an Agatha Christie or a Reader's Digest. Dad would be doing the crosswords or studying his book of Kipling's verse. When my father started reciting, Mum would get up and go for a walk. They surf in Tenby these days: I was back one Christmas recently and there were kids in wetsuits with surfboards. That was something new.

We'd also go and look at the big flying boat base at Pembroke Dock. The Australians were there—bronzed and tall in dark-blue uniforms, talking in funny voices. The Sunderlands were still operating services from Southampton to Australia and New Zealand and they continued to do so right up until the Constellations were introduced.

Tenby offered what most people wanted from a seaside resort in those days. When it was wet, parents could drag the kids along to Pembroke Castle to see where Henry VII was born and point out the English history. It's got Pendine Sands, where attempts were made on the land speed motor record in the 1920s and '30s by a mad Welshman, Parry Thomas, whose car blew up. Nearby, in Laugharne, there's Dylan Thomas's boat house where he wrote *Under Milk Wood* about this gossipy Welsh town. You could go out to Caldey Island on boats with names like *Saucy Sue*. Caldey has a monastery on it and it was wonderfully exciting for a child to look down from the top of the hill and see the monks moving about. They're still there, brewing some sort of Benedictine, which they sell.

Tenby is an English-speaking enclave in a Welsh-speaking area so that's why so many people from England have always gone there. It's tucked away, too. It's still relatively difficult to get there because there's only one motorway in Wales. Holidaymakers used to arrive by a single-decker bus—we always called it a charabanc—or on the train. The provincial railways went everywhere in those days, to all the tinpot villages in the country.

Tenby was paradise. It was as exotic to me then as all the tropical destinations I've seen as an adult—Tahiti, the Solomons. It's quite unlike those ghastly, decaying seafront places, such as Great Yarmouth, which are so depressing. My brother still has a caravan outside Tenby—he likes to walk along the cliffs. I've taken my wife, Robin, too, and she loves it. Last visit we saw some presentable looking mussels on the base of the jetty and we started scraping them off and a kid asked us what were we doing. We said we were going to eat them and he said we must be nuts. The water is heavily polluted with mercury and radioactive nuclear waste. The British have one of the most appalling records for dumping things in the ocean. If you caught a fish these days, it'd probably have three eyes! Anyway, we made a sort of bouillabaisse and, of course, we survived. It made me think of those boyhood days when we'd buy a paper cone of cockles or whelks for sixpence. They'd come with a pin so you could pick them out of the shell. Sometimes my father would turn to my mother and ask her for a brooch or a hairpin and he'd wander off, carefully picking at these tiny crustaceans. They tasted of the seaside.**99**

"Are we there yet, Dad?"

PAUL DYER
Musician

"When I was a young boy, my family used to rent a simple house during the Christmas school holidays, right on the beach, at Ettalong on the NSW Central Coast. These days, that area's very residential and parts of it are even fashionable—Pearl Beach is nearby—but back then it was off the beaten track: if you stopped off the highway, you'd see kangaroos.

The three Dyer children—myself, older sister Mary-ann and younger brother Anthony—would be *so* excited about the prospect of the journey. We lived in Pymble, on Sydney's upper North Shore, and we'd travel along the old Pacific Highway in our two-tone Holden sedan—lime-green and cream—with blue leather upholstery. The roof-racks would be piled high; each of us had a suitcase and there'd be the compulsory picnic basket with its plastic plates and cutlery and tartan tablecloth and serviettes. Even though it was hot and humid in January, we'd load up five crocheted blankets, hand-done by our Nanna with multi-coloured squares—one for each bed.

Mum, Eileen, would have nothing to do with the map. Dad, Bill, did all the work: the driving and the navigating. But that wouldn't stop Mum saying, 'You should have taken a right turning, not a left!' Dad would do precise preparations for the trip but Mum would be the decision-maker—what time we would be leaving and where we'd stop on the way—but together they had a great sense of fun. In the back, there'd be a constant chirping chorus of 'Are we there yet, Dad?' We'd play 'I Spy' and other time-filler games, and usually one of us would be in tears because we hadn't got our way over something!

My brother, being the youngest, always sat in the centre. In the old Holdens, there was quite a hump in the middle of the back floor so he'd have to put one leg each side, which must have been terribly uncomfortable when we were going around bends on that winding highway. He was always falling asleep onto me, or onto my sister on the other side; there was a hierarchy about who had which window. Dad would get very cranky if we put down the windows too far and it got too blowy. There was no air-conditioning in cars in those days and I remember a wonderful sense of freedom being on the road, on my way to the seaside, with the wind whipping my face and hair.

Just before we arrived at Ettalong, we'd stop for fresh bread and milk. I would feel a surge of excitement about being in a 'foreign' place with different shops and exotic summer fruit we didn't eat at home—mangoes, paw-paws, rockmelon, passionfruit.

We returned to the same cottage three times, because it was in a good location, close to all the amenities and, best of all, to the beach. It was fibro, it had a lawn, a hideous gate, a front fence with criss-crossed wire, like an institution. Mum would pick hydrangeas or geraniums from the garden and put them in vases, like a touch of home. It was a box, really, but it had quite a lot of rooms. There were two lounge rooms: one was skimpily covered with new but very thin carpet and the other had old-fashioned patterned lino of the sort that gathers every bit of dirt. There was a mulberry bush in the garden and the fruit would be on the ground, so often we trailed into the house with mucky purple feet.

After the first year, we decided all three children, plus our cousin, Gabrielle, who was the same age as my sister, would sleep in the same room. We'd be lined up in our little single beds—which were hard and uncomfortable—talking and giggling into the night. Or playing games: Monopoly, snap, poker. There was no TV but we were all keen readers, and sometimes I'd look up from my book and realise everyone was curled up, totally engrossed in what they were reading. It always seemed very warm and cosy. I loathed comics but I always had a Biggles book or an adventure story such as *Huckleberry Finn*. After the lights went out, I'd be aware of the sound of the fridge. It was a rickety old thing, with the freezer below—we'd have to go every other day to the petrol station and buy a block of ice for it—and it would shake and twitch all night.

After the holidays, I'd always find it hard to sleep the first few nights back in my own bed—I missed the sound of that fridge and the distant rolling of waves. There was a strange sense of loss and I wouldn't want my sunburn to fade. All summer, we'd have been basted with baby oil on the beach and we'd sizzle and fry; red skin was a badge of honour. You could show everyone what a good holiday you'd had by how burnt you were.

The Ettalong kitchen had all the basics but Mum always took her Mixmaster so she could make lemon cheese tarts. I'd be the one who whipped the lemon cheese—Philadelphia cream cheese, pure lemon and condensed milk—and Mum would do the pastry. She guarded the recipe as if it were a precious secret. For lunch, we'd have sandwiches, always on white bread, with devon and tomato sauce or drippy tinned asparagus. At five o'clock, we'd have to have a glass of milk but, because it was holiday time, we'd be allowed Paddle-pops at the beach. For tea, we'd *always* want fish and chips.

My sister had very sensitive skin, and my brother and I used to torment her like crazy: we knew if we slapped her on any part of the body, she would come up with our finger marks. It was a great holiday thing to slap Mary-ann! On the beach, we always had zinc cream lathered on our noses and new surf towels we'd got for Christmas—vibrant, fringed, patterned with Mexicans in huge hats, usually—and we wore hideous costumes. Because my brother and I looked like twins—although I was older and thought I was much more handsome!—we had the same clothing. I can remember wearing a brown velour bib-and-brace, which my brother also had to endure, and we must have looked like such dags.

Ettalong in those days was quiet. It's a flat place, not what you'd call beautiful. There's a lake just behind, a swampy tidal area, but the beach itself has a beautiful grain of sand. When you're young, you're very conscious of things like that: every beach has different sand. At Ettalong, the grains always seemed to me larger and coarser than the Sydney beaches and I found that quite exotic. We could dig our feet in the sand and dance the Watusi! It was so liberating to have bare feet after all those months at school in lace-up shoes. The water seemed much bluer than it did in Sydney and that added to the sense of being far away.

Because of the tides, the tangy marshy smell of the water was very strong. There was a wonderful rock pool but the movement of the tide would change how you felt about it, because if the tide was coming in, there'd be a sense of dare-devilry, whether you'd go out to the edge and dive into the rock pool as the tide came. It was pretty risky and a couple of times, I remember luring my brother out to this dangerous place and then leaving him stranded there.

We had a huge yellow-and-white umbrella we'd take onto the beach. We'd never stand it up with a proper pole but it'd be angled, like a shelter. We often had our photographs taken under or beside that umbrella—it was a totem of the holiday experience. Dad was a great body surfer and he'd ride the waves and Mum would be terribly colourful and vibrant on the sand, wonderfully uninhibited in her huge pleated swimsuit.

Those Ettalong days were a time of imagination, and wonder. I learned what it was to be with a family but to have a sense of aloneness, all at the same time. The days didn't have a firm structure, as they did at home, so you could escape a little bit, wander down to the end of the street and not know what was around the corner. The city was always a dangerous place, but Ettalong was safe. Except for sharks! There were lifesavers up on high chairs, always looking out to sea, and often the alarm would go, and out of the water we'd all race.

Despite that freedom, there was also a strange sense of urgency. We'd leap out of bed each morning and start pestering Dad: 'Come on, come on, come on, we've got to get to the beach!' Poor Dad probably wanted to potter around with the car or read the paper but we were too young to be considerate. This was *our* holiday. But there was always a great sense of family—often we'd have cousins with us or grandparents or elderly relatives and everyone would work out their daily ritual and then at night there'd be lots of talking and shared laughter.

Now, as an adult, constantly surrounded by sound, I look for solitude, which I can find by the sea. I find its rhythm very soothing, and in it are those happy childhood associations. I was very lucky to have those family holidays at Ettalong, full of innocence and wonderment and a sense of being alive and loved. **99**

You can take the boy out of Reservoir ...

BARRY DICKINS
Playwright

"Charles Dickens claimed to know every brick in London and I know every Fanta can in Melbourne. I know every tramline off by heart. I think I know what people are thinking, I think I am omniscient and I love and loathe it simultaneously—Melbourne, I mean. It is fabulous and dreary, it is finite and dead and so breezy. And there is a kindness in Melbourne.

The man over the road, his name is Michael, is a Greek, and he's retarded. He used to be a soccer star in Italy and last Christmas Day he came over, bouncing a soccer ball on his head, and smiled at me, meaning, 'Get the idea, we're going to play.' He gives roses to Sarah, my wife. Another fellow, Horace, who's 93, puts our mail under the front door. I can't imagine that happening in Kings Cross.

I remember the first time I was taken to the old heart of Melbourne. It was called 'going to town'. 'We're going to town,' was the mysterious offer. There was no railway station where we lived, you had to walk a mile to Reservoir, so called because of all the reservoirs there. It was a prosaic place—still is. It was a settlement town and after World War II, all the diggers tried to settle in. My father, Len, was one of them and I remember, as an infant, seeing men in demob clobber getting their front gardens going. My father ruptured his hernia hauling a cast-iron earth flattener—it was, in fact, an iron tennis court roller. Every time we went to the beach, he suffered a waterlogged hernia truss, making it impossible for him to go for a paddle. My mother, Edna, would be calling out, 'C'mon, Len, you're missing out on the water.' What could he do? They don't ever dry out.

My grandmother's name was Gert and she lived in West

Preston—Miller Street—and I often went to stay with her but I loved her sister, Bessie, better. I've often written about them, they were my heroes. Gert was a bit like my mother, she made everything special, like cutting open a cantaloupe in a special way, all zig-zaggedy.

I'd sometimes accompany my grandmother to the phone box when she was teeing up a meeting with Bessie. I was a child, waiting outside the phone box—I'm going back 42 years—but I remember the lovely dark green glass and standing with my nose pressed up against it. And my grandmother would be on tiptoe because she wasn't really tall enough to reach the 'talk bit' and the 'listen thing'. There was a black Bakelite circle, it had a thing on the side with A and B buttons, on an angle, and I think the call cost two pennies. You rolled the pennies to the right and spoke. I suppose you could call it working-class magic.

She used to hit the button and the pennies would go down together. You'd dial the code, then the number and it would go through to Noble Park and you'd hear Bessie pick it up with a 'Yeasss' and then 'You there?' and my grandmother would hit the button, and the sound sort of amplified. You had to be quick to push the button. And then she'd say, 'It's me. How are ya? All right . . . Are we gunna meet? . . . Yeasss. Righto. See you then . . .'

And then they would meet at Flinders Street Station, under the clocks. But they'd never give each other a day or time. Sometimes they'd foil each other and turn up an hour earlier or later. Occasionally, simultaneously, they'd meet up on the wrong day.

The first time I went to town with my grandmother, we got the train from Thornbury. She gave me a morning in the city, walking past St Paul's Cathedral, listening to the chiming old bells. There were seats outside St Paul's and I ate an orange and watched the drunks go past, feeling protected by her. She took me to Myer, where they used to have the most fantastic peppermint ice cream, and then to Flinders Street Station. In those days, they had an amazing weighing machine which you stood on and my grandmother would dial the letters. This creaking would start up inside the machine and it'd give you a brass plate with your name embossed on it. There wasn't anything you could do with it except wear it around your neck!

I'd come from a place of paddocks and grass seeds and I was overwhelmed by Melbourne's grace and noble architecture. We walked up Swanston Street, through the summer crowds, my grandmother holding my hand—she was so strong!—looking at the Manchester Unity Building and all those sparrows chirping away in the portico of the Town Hall. An intellectual aviary.

We walked up Little Collins Street and she said, 'Look down there, that's where they keep the workers.' It looked like a series of windows, set in the footpath, and she told me the workers got thruppence worth of light a day. She was always Geiger-countering away as she walked along, looking for detail, and I picked that up from her.

We didn't go to town often so it was always special. I remember seeing Catholic girls walking down Collins Street with their gloves on, because their mothers insisted they wore them to town—and probably ironed them first. People dressed up in those days: Melbourne isn't special like that any more. The other day, I saw two girls shooting up in a doorway during office hours and it made me realise how much things have changed. It shocked me, because of the time: if it had been before or after work, it wouldn't have surprised me, because you see it everywhere. It hurt me to see them so casual about it. It was only 10 am. A bit early for heroin, I thought, but it isn't funny.

On my twelfth birthday, my father took me to see *Oliver* at the Princess Theatre, and before the show he took me to an archaic hotel called the New Treasury, which has since been demolished, unfortunately. It was overwhelming for me and I cried because everything seemed so historic, pendulous and heavy. I'd never seen such heavy silverware. Back at home, we ate our tea on white Woolworth's plates with Woolworth's knives and forks.

And the smell of the damask and heavy linen and candles set on the table—there was a big candle between my father and myself and it was only about 6.30 in the evening. My father ordered me a Porterhouse and the woman laughed at me because I'd never had a steak. He wanted the very best for me but it was all too much and I think I spoiled it for him. He took me to the Windsor Hotel. He had a beer and I had a lemon squash with a little umbrella in it. Standing at the bar together, all I could see was his belt.

Reservoir had a lot of housing commission flats and while I was growing up it was violent, with street fights, and extreme poverty. People rode pushbikes, sometimes without tyres on them. An early form of gaffer tape was wrapped around them. When men broke the front forks on their push-bikes, they improvised and used forked branches and often I saw blokes riding bikes around with newspapers for tyres, with wire tied around the newspaper to keep it in place.

My mum and dad and elder brother, John, still live in the

old double-brick home I was born in. It's extremely strong, that brick veneer house. An electrician came one day to drill into the walls to put in new wiring and his drills snapped in half.

There was no swimming pool in Reservoir, there was one at Preston which was three miles away. If folks wanted to go to the beach, they had to catch a series of trains. The beach train was holy! Our house was in Rathcown Road and we'd walk the mile to Reservoir Station, where we'd queue up and buy some sort of extension ticket, the top half was pink. It'd be so hot and breathless and we waited an eternity for the dusty red rattler to come into the station. Working people going for a swim, some of them tram conductresses, bus drivers, the ones who served the community having their day off, and that used to get to me, seeing the varicose veins of the tram conductresses under their torn stockings, their exhaustion, their eagerness to go for a swim.

We'd stop at Thornbury Station to pick up my grandmother and she'd be waiting there and the kids would be clawing to get out of the hot carriage. It was like a dim sum container full of steamed citizens. We had bags with our togs in them—we never called them bathers, even the women referred to them as togs: 'You got your togs on under your dress?'

When I think of the amount of stuff we used to take to the beach, like a collapsible badminton set with screw-in poles held together by butterfly clips, it was made of silver plastic, and we'd carry all this junk—plastic transparent golf sets and magic tricks to entertain the crowds on the train.

I always knew how to play the room. I had this rubber lemon with a hole and you could stuff a silk handkerchief into it so it looked like the handkerchief had turned into a lemon. The whole community would be in this carriage. There was Mr Mack, the draper, who taught me how to do a top spin backhand at tennis, a guy who succeeded in growing the only pineapple in Reservoir, another who had a kangaroo. The Reverend W. Stelling, going for a swim in his dog collar, choking himself with it. There was a fairly wealthy Aboriginal family, which in the '40s and '50s was unbelievable in Reservoir. The father was physically very beautiful and you'd see him neatly mowing his lawn with a push-pull mower. He was a public servant, so you can imagine how he stood out among the calico shirts and prejudices.

We'd rattle into the city, off to Prince's Bridge, walk across Swanston Street, and you had your extension ticket to go on to the beach towns. They had exotic or rather flat names, depending on your whimsy, like Brighton Beach or Carrum, Sandringham, Mordialloc. I've always liked the name Mordialloc, sounds like someone's nose getting caught in a zipper. If we were a bit broke, we'd get out at Carrum. If we had a bit more dough, we would go to Black Rock, which was more remote. But just as awful, or wonderful. Everything was appalling and wondrous.

There was no surf at any of the beaches, just sort of tattered unemployed waves. It was the pure joy of running along the sand and through the rock pools. My father always liked Black Rock because it had stonefish and if you stood on one, you died. In the early 1950s, that's exactly what happened to a Pom and my father always liked Black Rock after that.

My father was, and still is, a good sportsman. He used to put up the badminton set with the long poles, mark up the court with his foot in the sand and we'd play, sometimes with a plastic ball with holes drilled through it which floated in the wind, and these cork-tipped bats or plastic paddles which were blue and red and rather heavy when you hit the feather against the wind, a plastic feather with a red tip. A sacred game. Our badminton Dreaming.

Sometimes he would take us to his battalion reunion, Christmas parties which were called gymkhanas, and they were held at Sandringham. They were a misery to me and a wonder, like everything else in my life, because the cricket was played on the hard packed sand after the men got drunk at the barbecue. The cricket was violent and they used things like a rotten bit of driftwood for a cricket bat. It was a very unwieldy instrument to hit a tennis ball with. The diggers played dead set and there were violent appeals for LBW, and the women not being able to get involved in it, and trying to hit a skun tennis ball all the way to Westernport, which was the idea, down on one knee trying to be a gladiator.

A length of special sand would be marked off for a treasure hunt and the adults would bury coupons under the sand. Someone would fire a cap gun and the children would run around this roped-off area and, if you discovered a coupon, it could be redeemed at the kiosk for an ice cream or chocolate-coated nuts. I remember crying at the age of three because I couldn't find a coupon. I was terrified I wouldn't get a lolly or an orange icy pole and then some old digger shuffled in the sand with his thong, revealed the edge of a coupon and prodded it up on his big toenail. I was in tears and I think I wet myself. Pipeline Petes had come in and I really wanted one. They were the best icy poles ever made.

There was this fantastic thing of smells, too, connected to the sand. Coconut oil, the smell of shell grit or wet tennis balls, it is like Mass for me, not growing up Catholic but growing up guilty. It was incredibly physical.

I saw a man get into a fist fight at Brighton Beach once, because he trod on someone's fruitcake tin—you know the deep noise you make when you stand on a fruitcake tin? And some guy saying, 'Did you step on my mother's fruitcake tin? You're gone!' People set up their checked and tasselled picnic rugs on the sand and woe betide anyone who accidentally trod on the edge of one—a fruitcake tin defined it. It was their sand. There was something very ungenerous about it all.

We Dickins boys made our own fun, which we were good at. I grew up with three brothers: John, the eldest, myself, Chris and Robert, all about three years apart. My father could make us cry with laughter by just looking at him. A great untrained clown. He was always reading to us, even at the beach, very persuasively. He was a great reciter, not in that boombiddy, boombiddy boom style but in a measured way. He'd read and read, and interpret books for his children so that literature was available to us, a part of the beach.

My place in the heart of Australia was some sort of eternal guarantee of joy and laughter, health and happiness—all of it rendered faithfully by our leader, my father. If anything remotely sorrowful was afoot, my mother would give it the heave-ho, saying, 'Too sad!'

I was lucky to be born into a very excited—over-excited you may say—buoyant, good home that laughed and wept and went to bed of a night with a brainful of stories to unravel in comic and tragic dreams of the everyday. Raymond Carver wouldn't have got a word in at our family tea time.**"**

A toast to
the coast

SARINA BRATTON
Businesswoman

"I was born and bred by the sea and grew up within walking distance of Australia's most famous beach— Sydney's Bondi. But every September, we packed up the station wagon and headed north for three weeks. Our destination was Kingscliff, a quaint seaside town well off the tourist trail and only half an hour south of the Queensland border. It's an idyllic seaside spot with a small hotel and a few shops on the seafront strip, the most important of which, to us, was the bakery. Our holiday cabin was separated from huge rolling sandhills and crashing surf by a roadway and a river ran down to the beach area which was a great area for my elder sister, Sharyn, and I to play. We'd catch the odd fish there, too.

Mum and Dad had good friends, John and Molly O'Grady, who would stay at Cabarita which is fairly close to Kingscliff. John had written *They're a Weird Mob*; a few years earlier it was Mum who'd introduced Molly to John and then they'd married. My parents and the O'Gradys would often meet in the pub for a drink in the late afternoon or early evening and Sharyn and I would have a pink lemonade. Often there'd be men near the hotel selling huge mud crabs which we'd buy and take back to the cabin to cook.

The journey up to Kingscliff was always packed with excitement as we motored up the old Pacific Highway in our Holden station wagon, which would be packed to the hilt. We'd stop at Nabiac for coffee. I usually managed to become terribly car sick but Dad had the perfect cure. As soon as we hit the sugar belt, he would pull the car over to the side of the road and cut me a huge piece of cane. Then I'd suck on this for hours—it seemed to have quite magical medicinal qualities—

27

or trail it out the window like an oversized baton. When I wasn't sucking, I'd be singing—those drives from Sydney were often one long sing-along.

We generally stopped overnight at a roadside motel at Port Macquarie or Kempsey. It was a big deal to have dinner at the motel restaurant as our family didn't eat out very often in those days. And my sister and I thought it was great not having to make our own beds. We loved the room-service breakfast—the novelty of bacon and eggs shoved through a funny little serving hatch on a tray.

Our arrival at Kingscliff was preceded by almost unbearable excitement. As we holidayed there every year, we had come to know the locals and many of the regular visitors and we always looked forward to seeing them again—it was like one big family. Our home-away-from-home was a small wooden cabin and it was wonderful for Mum as she could blithely sweep the sand straight out the front door. There were five or six cabins in the complex where we stayed and ours had two bedrooms, kitchen, bathroom and living area. The decor was that of a real holiday flat, with no carpet and no precious ornaments to break.

Sharyn and I spent each long, perfect day surfing, swimming and tumbling on the sand. Dad always packed our bikes and my favourite chore was to rise very early and ride into town to buy just-baked bread and fresh milk, which in those days came in bottles. My enthusiasm for this daily excursion invariably landed me in trouble, however, because I could never resist tucking into the bread, fingers first, before returning to the cabin. It was as close to heaven as a young girl could get to be riding along with the smell of fresh bread assailing my nostrils, the sound of waves breaking on shore,

the warm sun on my face and the melodious song of the cur-
rawongs or the cackle of kookaburras ringing in the air.

Mum and Dad joined Sharyn and me at the beach most
days. We'd go fishing, with Dad putting the bait on our hooks.
My hair would be bleached white and I'd soon be as brown as
a nut. Every day was jam-packed with activities; I don't think
Sharyn and I ever stopped running and we'd be whacked by
the time evening came. But we always had energy left for a
game of cards. There was no TV but we'd listen to the radio,
read and talk—lots of good old-fashioned communication.

At the time I was a competitive diver and gymnast, so
when not surfing, I spent much of each day tumbling and
training on the beach. In September 1968, however, I took
time out to lounge on my beach-towel and listen to reports
of the Mexico Olympic Games on my radio. Sue Knight was
the Australian diving representative at the Games and she was
my idol. Her coach was Jack Barnett who also used to teach
me in my early days of dive training. The next year, I was to
become the Australian junior one metre and highboard champion as well as the Australian junior and open trampoline
champion. I'd also won various state medals in diving, gymnastics and trampolining and everyone seemed amazed I
could achieve in three different sports.

Those years have had such a tremendous influence on me
that my husband, Ray, and I now intend to plan a similar holiday ritual with our daughter, Bianca, to the same place at the
same time every year. We hope this will provide her with
equally happy memories and will teach her the importance of
simple pleasures.

I still live and holiday by the sea. Ray and I have a boat
and we spend our spare time catching up with friends at

Pittwater and on the Hawkesbury River or at Port Stephens. We don't have TV on the boat but we do have fishing rods, canoes, books, cards, a few clothes and sleeping bags. It's a great family time with lots of laughs and lots of friends. We make our own enjoyment—just like the Kingscliff days—and that might mean taking the dinghy or kayak for an exploratory cruise to observe sea eagles or just singing our heads off.

Although my work takes me all over the world, when I think 'beach holiday', I think Australia. There's a wonderfully wild element to our beaches which really sets them apart. The surf is different, the sand much softer and finer, and the water's a singular colour. The Pacific Ocean, in particular, differs from anything you might see around the Mediterranean or on the east coast of the USA. Recently, I was in Florida and desperate to feel the sand between my toes but the beaches were a tremendous disappointment; they seem so contained and developed and false.

In Australia you need never travel far to find a beautiful and usually deserted beach. Sydney's northern beaches, for example, are quite lovely and wild and more-or-less empty. My favourites include Lighthouse Beach near Seal Rocks in northern NSW—it's a long climb down through a range of sand hills but well worth it—and Port Stephens on NSW's mid-north coast. We generally potter about in our boat near the entrance to the harbour, exploring the islands, dropping anchor to swim ashore and have lunch on the beach.

Having a daughter has given me the opportunity to get back in touch with my own happy childhood memories. Those September days by the sea were, quite simply, among the happiest of my life. 99

Endless
horizons

KATE LLEWELLYN
Writer

"I was born at Tumby Bay, a little town on the west coast of South Australia. Matthew Flinders sailed up this coastline and named all the locations after places in Lincolnshire, which was his county. It's just a little fishing village, really; Port Lincoln is the main port for all the region—it's wheat and wool country. Although it has a very, very low rainfall, it is rich agriculturally. It's certainly not a tourist resort—I wouldn't tell anyone to buy a ticket and go—but it's a very special place for my family.

One of the best things about going back is that it feels the same—so few things have changed. There are pelicans now, which weren't there in my childhood, a caravan park and a few more buildings. It's got a famous jetty which the residents barricaded for weeks and saved when it was to be pulled down. My father used to come ashore at the jetty from sailing. The tennis courts where my parents used to play are still there.

My father opened the Tumby Bay Elder Smith's Stock and Station firm in the 1930s and that business survives today. My mother had come from the Barossa Valley so they moved to Tumby Bay after their honeymoon and I was born there a year later. It's the palest and most bleached landscape. There is just nothing bright. The cloudless, arching sky covers the great empty space like a blue teacup upside down on a cream saucer. It couldn't be more of a contrast to, say, Sydney, with its colours of hibiscus. All the trees in the desert have thin leaves and that was what astonished me about Sydney—the wide-leafed plants. Tumby Bay is all pastels—the white and cream of daisy bushes which once grew along the shore and a pale, pale sea, quite turquoise like tropical waters. You can see your toenails, you can see the fish. There are a lot of sharks so the sea, to me, has always had elements of both ravishing beauty and great danger. Sometimes there'd be white pointer sharks hanging at the end of the jetty, which gave an exciting, almost nightmarish feeling.

The swings and slippery dips of my childhood are still there—the same ones. They were built to last. It was an idyllic childhood: sand, sea and daisy bushes and a hot, arid climate always relieved by a cool afternoon breeze. I also had the benefits of country town living where one's parents were loved and respected. Being the first child of a dressmaker mother, I was always dressed in beautiful smocked Liberty fabrics and viyellas. I was a white-haired, cosseted little fop.

However, I had three brothers so a lot of the bliss disappeared when they came. Those boys made my life difficult. I saw a photo the other day which a magazine had blown up and I thought, 'That little girl looks absolutely beleaguered.' It was me; my mouth looks so drawn—I was probably at my wits' end. They were physically stronger than me. I couldn't beat them in fights. I was very jealous of them because they came along and spoiled my love affair with my parents. I think Eden was meant to be ruined: that's its fate.

Tumby Bay is a wonderful place to visit still. There's a little pub at the end of the jetty, which my godmother once owned. It has a long Chinese Chippendale balcony looking out to sea. I went there about five years ago and thought I'd have a bath upstairs in the shared bathroom. I ran the water and had it up to my neck. The next morning I went downstairs for breakfast and the owner asked, 'Did you enjoy your bath?' I replied, 'Indeed I did, Cassie.' She said, 'So did we, because the insurance company is going to be called in now. The plumbing wasn't connected and your bath has ruined the bottom room.'

We flew to Adelaide every year for our father's annual holidays. Even though we hadn't been in trams or trains until we were 10 or 12, we had always been in planes. That's one of my earliest memories. We took up the whole plane and my mother always had someone help to take care of us. My brothers were always vomiting into paper bags. There was an air hostess with very smart legs and a hat—that's how we travelled. It was too far to travel any other way because with children you just couldn't drive that distance.

We left Tumby Bay when my father was given another posting. My mother broke the news in front of people at afternoon tea. She just said, 'By the way, we are going to move.' I burst into tears and my mother laughed and said, 'Look, she's crying.' She didn't mean to be unkind, but I was absolutely speechless because I couldn't imagine another place to live.

So now we all go back to Tumby Bay and take photographs and make sketches. I bought raddle from Elder Smith's— raddle is the chalk you mark sheep with—and kept it for years. So we are all very nostalgic and ridiculous about it. My eldest brother has had the old house sketched and has had photographs blown up and framed.

Tumby Bay has had an effect on the way my brothers and I live. For instance, the whole family is keen on space. With the exception of myself, we each have a large house with big rooms. My brothers all have dining room tables the size of billiard tables, and my mother was always knocking down walls to enlarge rooms. As soon as we moved into a place, she would say, 'That has to go and that has to go!' There were always men knocking down, opening up, creating space.

As a result, we also have very large, emotional lives—lots of melodrama, I think. One brother owns sheep and cattle stations. He's buying adjoining stations to get to the sea—he builds drains 19 kilometres long. I think that desire really comes from playing a childhood game in which we used quandong stones for sheep and pegs for railing. The desert quandong tree was to us as the olive is to the Greeks. It gave us our fruit and shade, and the seeds were our toys. We laid the pegs flat on the carpet, and on the few rainy days we had, that's what we played. It's very easy to enlarge your property if you have a packet of pegs—you can just keep going on and on until you run out of the room. I think we all have that feeling that we can just keep going—into the hall, the street, across the whole continent.

Recently, I was in Western Australia going north and I felt, 'I really don't want to turn around, there's Indonesia over there, it's only 400 kilometres ahead. All you need is a boat and you can just keep going.' The same in Africa. I was going up the east coast of Tanzania with a driver and a cook and after Tanga—a perhaps once-beautiful town colonised by the Germans and Arabs—I kept thinking, I could get to Ethiopia if I just keep going. It was with the greatest reluctance I turned back. I suppose the fact that there were wars up there had an effect on me.

The most perfect way to travel is with a cook and driver. No one else. Just go—I did it that way in Africa and India.

I love a flat horizon and I find it extraordinary that people can say, 'Oh there's nothing here!' To me, it is like a wire fence that you can ping and it's practically a feeling of electricity in the air, because it's so tense in its emptiness. All this is linked to my interest in Australian deserts. I'm just finishing a book about them, called *Swags: In Footsteps of Australian Explorers*. What I think is interesting about an Australian childhood near the coast is that—with a few noble exceptions—people look towards the sea and rarely turn and face inland. But the interior is where it's really exciting. It never occurred to any of us to look behind. I'm very interested in the 19th-century explorers so I've taken trips in the footsteps of Giles, Sturt, Burke and Wills. And Len Biddell, the great 20th-century explorer.

Biddell made the 'bomb roads' through South Australia, so called because they brought in the British scientists to make the atomic bomb tests at Maralinga and Emu. Some of those roads I think will shortly be closed to the public but I've been lucky enough to go on them. They are simply red tracks which he named after members of his family—there's the Anne Biddell Highway and the Connie-Sue, who was their baby at the time. The baby had a bath in a bucket once a fortnight. Out there there's almost no water, apart from the occasional native well, and a couple of newly dug wells which travellers now have access to. Then I went on further, following Giles up the centre of Western Australia to the Canning Stock Route, which is another great feat of Australian exploration. It will possibly be closed shortly because Aboriginal people who own the land will be happy not to have people running over it. In a lot of these places you have to have permission to go there, but I was with my brother, Bill Brinkworth, who runs South Australian Outback Bush Adventures. He takes people professionally so he had permits.

I went to the Simpson Desert with Bill. It's a nine-day trip from Adelaide to the largest set of parallel red sand dunes in the world. All day, you feel like a ship at sea on the red sand going across and across until you get to Birdsville and the famous Birdsville Pub. I really hate ceilings after trips like that because they cut out the stars. When you just have a swag, you can become very attached to that way of living. It's an immense privilege to travel in the Outback. The land is so fragile, every time you put your foot down, you feel it's winning. The plants are so delicate, beautiful and bizarre.

Another desert which is one of Australia's best-kept secrets is Lawn Hill National Park, 250 kilometres north of Mt Isa. It's brilliant and I think better to visit than Kakadu, although it's not nearly as famous. It has a river through gorges down which you can canoe to wonderful waterfalls. You can stand behind these waterfalls and watch from water caves. It's a very ravishing place. It's near there that the great fossil finds in Riverslea on the Gregory River were made in the 1980s. In fact, there's a huge fossil-finding industry there. Great extinct animals have been discovered.

It's beautifully run by Queensland National Parks. At Lawn Hill, visitors must move camp every second night. You aren't allowed to stay very long and certainly not allowed to camp on the same piece of grass for longer than 48 hours so it's a very pristine landscape. The second time I went in there were tears running down my face. I couldn't really tell you why, but it's just so beautiful. One doesn't like to cry in front of strangers.

I have also followed the steps of Thomas Mitchell to Carnarvon and Burke and Wills up to Coopers Creek. I've been doing a lot of travel in Sturt's footsteps. He is one of the greatest inland explorers because he was holed up for six months through the heat of summer and survived brilliantly. I'm just very drawn, I think, to immense danger. There is a quote from Sturt about this in his journal, saying that they were as cut off as they'd be in Antarctica.

The explorers' women stayed at home and they, too, were brave, immensely brave. The danger of these deserts is still there and of course plenty of people have died because of their ignorance. So I think a landscape that's beautiful and dangerous really draws me—especially if it has a great flat horizon. 99

Chapter 2

THIS IS *MY* PLACE

Australians in love with a special spot Down Under

Where the stars
are lit by neon

GRAEME BLUNDELL
Actor

"A piece of poetry by Kenneth Slessor had stuck in my brain for years. I don't know where or when I first read it but somehow it always came to mind when I thought of Sydney. It was about Kings Cross, or maybe Darlinghurst, next door—that wonderfully seedy, romantic precinct:

> Where the stars are lit by neon
> Where the fried potato fumes
> And the ghost of Mr Villion
> Still inhabits single rooms
> And the girls lean out from Heaven
> Over lightwells, thumping mops . . .
> While the gent in 57
> Cooks his pound of mutton chops.

In the neon madness of the Cross, wandering its square mile of fugitive hilltop, you enter a world where you can reinvent yourself in the casual act of hanging around. In the mid-'60s, Slessor wrote that it was curious, haunting, exciting and brassy, 'a mixture of Montmartre, Chelsea, Greenwich Village, Port Said and Reno transplanted to the Southern Hemisphere.'

That's why I moved there in 1979. I loved the idea of layer upon layer of humanity living and loving and suffering, exulting or dying in what Slessor referred to as 'the great antheap of its brick and concrete'. I loved thinking that I was seeing what he had seen as he walked home from the newspaper where he worked in the 1940s and '50s. These were the same streets that Lennie Lower had made into comedy, that Dorothy Hewett has transformed to poetry. People would point out where Chips Rafferty had lived over a butcher's shop, Charmian Clift and George Johnston had fought and fornicated, Peter Finch had read to the prostitutes in Palmer Street—his first paying job as an actor, it was said—and Bill Hunter had thrown a cop, or so it was rumoured, through a plate glass window.

The Cross had lived in my imagination for years. I would stay there briefly on visits from Melbourne in the late-'60s—it was a tapestry of rock and roll, flared clothes, underground publications, communal experiments and being kind to each other over sitar music and herbal tea. Sex with strangers was little more disreputable than violence on TV.

I can remember wandering around the corner from St Vincents [Hospital] in the early '70s and going to Brett Whiteley openings at Kym Bonython's Paddington gallery. They were happenings, really; highly contrived showbiz events. I loved the way people were asked to communicate with the space and each other as well as the paintings. It was art as performance, articulated and animated. And I took these fantastical visions back to greyer, more serious Melbourne. I recall Donald Friend saying that, yes, all that stuff about Tinsel Town and Sin City was quite true. Sydney was extroverted, he said, and had never gone in all that much for sobriety: 'Well, dignity can have its headquarters as long as it's got a blue suit.'

I loved the Yellow House [the artists' colony started by Martin Sharp] in Challis Avenue, painted in orange, red, black and blue, and you could never tell where the decoration stopped and the art began. You could walk to it through the Cross in the sunlight under the plane trees in Victoria Street, or along Darlinghurst Road, past the Crazy Horse bar, curry houses, laundromats, hippie poster shops, and the three-storey terraces with their lace balconies and ornate chimney pots. There was always the smell of roasting coffee and the patisseries would be full of fresh cakes and the delis bursting with Swedish herring rolls, a thousand smoky wursts and beautifully packaged boxes of Viennese sugar almonds.

Hare Krishna monks floated past, suspended in yards of apricot cotton, chanting their cheerful mantras, bobbing and weaving through the streets. Macleay Street was so cosmopolitan you could believe it was paved with gold—the expensive cars had tinted windows, there were limousines parked in front of the Chevron Hotel, the frock shops had begun to call themselves boutiques and there were serious stores with huge plate-glass windows full of shining Georgian silver. I can recall Ruth Park describing Texan tourists speaking with 'the dry burr of rattlesnakes' as they invested in gold-framed landscape paintings and 'pocketfuls of under-priced Australian gems.'

For years, doing TV and making films, I stayed at the Sebel Town House in Elizabeth Bay Road. It was just across the road from a terminally brown, scungy apartment block where I'd first slept with a Sydney girl called Christine in a tiny room that had no cupboards and a plague of cockroaches. Like so many rooms in Kings Cross, when you entered it at night and switched on the light, the whole place appeared to be moving.

The Sebel was a legend. The rooms weren't all that flash but each carried great history. Who else had slept in this bed? You knew you could behave outrageously at the Sebel and they wouldn't throw you out. A producer friend stayed there during her wedding. 'Three extra chairs, a roll of gaffer tape, piles of sandwiches and order a taxi to pick up the bridesmaid's missing shoes,' she trumpeted down the phone, fazing no one. Coming out of the best man's room at 6 am after the last bottle of champagne, she and her new husband bumped into an elderly American tourist. 'You've kept me awake all night,' she said to them. 'But you're obviously having a great time so I'm doing my laundry.'

The Sebel Bar was dangerous then. Actors were known to disappear there—it was a sort of Bermuda Triangle for careers! The air was always yeasty and full of smoke and everyone would be waiting for the rock stars to turn up after their gigs. None of the women ever appeared to be completely dressed and they drank from glasses full of pink foam, decorated with paper umbrellas. The bar didn't close until the last customer left—people would be lurching up to the Bourbon and Beefsteak for breakfast. We used to reckon the old actors' joke originated at the Sebel Bar: 'You're not really drunk if you can still lie on the floor without hanging on.'

The more intrepid of actors would hang out at the Venus Room in Orwell Street, just down from Actors' Equity. A huge bouncer would check you out at the door—to make sure you weren't a cop—and there was a short-order kitchen doing food for drunks—fried eggs and greasy hamburgers— and a bar the length of an entire wall. Near-naked girls danced on top of tables and in cages. Go go girls for ga ga men! I can remember having the most impassioned talks about the nature of acting in this seediest of environments.

When I actually moved to the Cross, I put an attic into the terrace I eventually bought in Surrey Street, just off Victoria Street. From this top room you could see towering Centrepoint; its spire was a beacon in a hazy vista of powder blue sky. After dark, the skyline was lit up like a jukebox and messages appeared mysteriously overnight on the bitumen footpaths: Welcome To Wherever You Are.

I'd ended up in Surrey Street by accident: the little Nimrod Theatre was at the end of Nimrod Street, which ran off Surrey Street, parallel to Victoria Street, and I'd admired the work of Ken and Lilian Horler and John Bell and others at the Nimrod and had spent many pleasurable hours with Ken in the bar afterwards. We often ate before shows at the Belgrade Inn in Surrey Street—nowhere in Sydney served up a better skewered continental sausage. One day on the way to rehearsal, Ken and I climbed over the back fence, like a couple of robbers in skivvies, of a terrace which Ken had heard was for sale. It appeared derelict and there were so many chokos on vines we could barely see the house—at least Ken told me they were chokos, I'd never seen one in Melbourne. They looked like psychedelic green coconuts. It wasn't a terribly romantic start to the association I was to have with the house for 14 years.

There were squatters on the bend of Surrey Street, a soup kitchen for down-and-outers down the way. Brothels stretched along Victoria Street and parts were very seedy—they used to say you could walk three blocks [in Kings Cross] without leaving the scene of the crime. But the coffee shops were full of actors and writers. There was the Tropicana where the Nanas [the recovering addicts from Narcotics Anonymous] used to sit in the morning sun, drinking coffee; the Formula One coffee bar; the Cafe Nicolina; La Bussola, where the house special was a fiery pizza called L'Inferno, and the San Remo, where local detective novelists liked to sit, inventing plots as a parade of characters who must surely have escaped from fiction wandered past. Sometimes, famous literary critics would be sitting in the gutter outside the Coluzzi nursing small cups of strong black coffee, gazing mournfully into space.

The waitresses were beautiful and looked as if they were waiting for a drug baron to ask them to run away . . . I remember talking to a young woman who looked like Stevie Nicks in the San Remo coffee shop. She lived in a communal household in Little West Street at the back of Darlinghurst. A musician, she was waitressing between gigs. She explained to me her group marriage—three men and seven women—had turned out to be the answer to the failures of Christian unions. 'How long has it worked out so well?' I asked. 'Since last Tuesday,' she replied.

The plane trees in Victoria Street seemed to whisper, telling their secrets of the past while the gargoyles on the tops of the buildings stood watch; walking down that wide, beautiful, shady street, I'd always think of the green bans on demolition, the barricades around the deteriorating houses, the single gas burners sitting on top of laminex tables in the corners of bachelor rooms. I'd always think of the [still-unsolved] disappearance of Juanita Neilsen, the heiress activist who campaigned against high-rise developments.

At Surrey Street in the summer, I loved the way the insinuating heat rose around the house, the exhausted evening air, the sense of the city being petrified as dark settled. The nights laden with layers of Kings Cross meaning. There was water, too. Everywhere you walked around Darlinghurst, there was water gleaming in all directions: harbour views suddenly catching you as you abruptly turned a corner or left a tatty apartment block, and then your heart would catch in your throat as Sydney's shimmery unreality enveloped you.

There were times, though, when it could seem like a huge

concrete garage. Cars everywhere and it was impossible to park—even tour buses and lorries filling the footpaths. A rat's maze of space in which to walk. Sometimes the streets were so busy, especially the famous intersection at the top of William Street, that my kids would say that the only way to get across was to be born on the other side.

My agent was ten minutes' walk down William Street towards the city. Shanahan Management was started by the late Bill Shanahan. Modest and unassuming, Bill had a loathing of big-noters, snobbery, intrigue and long lunches. He worked tirelessly to promote and protect the interests of his clients, vet their scripts and guard their secrets. He had a way of letting you know it was all right to have a good time and be intensely serious as well. The City Gym was another landmark, full of actors of every sexual persuasion. There was only one rule: on no account must a participant in an aerobics class be better turned out than the instructor. Grave humiliation always resulted from such presumption.

Just up the street, Kinselas started as a clearing-house for alternative comedy and I helped turn the old funeral parlour into a production company creating teen dreams for the over-thirties. Kinselas is where I learned that producing is like sex: you never see anyone else doing it and you're never sure if you're doing it right!

I left the Cross in 1996 for Stanmore in the inner-west of Sydney. I still live in a terrace, there's a city skyline view from the top balcony—fireworks over Centrepoint on New Year's Eve—and it's only 10 minutes by car to the Cross. But I joke to all my friends that I've gone to live in the country. **"**

Kakadu
Dreaming

STEVE PARISH
Photographer and publisher

"Kakadu is fantastic. It's tropical woodlands, buffaloes, crocodile encounters, and being surrounded by tens of thousands of birds. It's being out on the floodplain in the dry season when the first storm comes and seeing parched land with huge cracks just drinking the water, and standing naked in it, and running around like a three-year-old. Dozens of experiences. Crawling through the ancient stone country of Arnhem Land Plateau where soil has eroded, leaving out-crops and overhangs of stone and rock, and discovering rock art galleries that probably haven't been visited by Aborigines or Europeans for hundreds of years. Or going out to the stone country in a helicopter and being lifted above Jim Jim Falls. Or wandering around in the peak of the wet when everything is really beautiful. You don't have those magnificent experiences in, say, the Dandenongs of Victoria—not the same grandeur, a different kind of beauty.

I first went to Kakadu in 1978. I was working for Queensland National Parks and Wildlife Services as a photographer. There was an international training program on there, and they had the head rangers from places like Nepal, the USA and South America. A fellow called Ian Morris was their guide, taking them around Australia. Ian was a great influence on me. He had holidayed on Elcho Island and known Arnhem Land Aborigines from childhood. He spoke the dialects and was an interesting manager—a born-again Christian who also embraced Aboriginal culture, which I knew to be very different to, say, our Christian culture. He gave a talk and waxed lyrical about the awesome majesty of this space that was filled with life—one hundred thousand magpie geese taking off in a flock, flood plains literally covered with birds.

I'd never appreciated that in Australia there was a natural environment that supported such wildlife. There's something like five hundred and fifty species of birds at Kakadu. It's got mammals and reptiles which are endemic only to that area— rock pigeon, black wallaroo and Oenpelli python, just to mention a few.

That was what first attracted me. I took six weeks' leave from my job with National Parks and did a private trip: ventured up across the border in a beat-up old Landrover with a friend of mine and we camped around the billabongs in Kakadu. We pulled in at Nourlangie Billabong and stayed in an empty house. I found out that very first night how welcome the house was because the mosquitoes around those billabongs are absolutely staggering. You can squeeze the air and come out with a bloody hand. We stayed there for what was to be a fortnight and left six weeks later. In the contract photography work I'd done prior to this trip, I'd only stayed a very short time and moved on. I fell for the whole idea of staying in one place and really getting to know it—where the birds were moving, which bank and what time of day the crocodiles sunned themselves. I found myself going feral, if you like, and smelled of sweat. It was October and very hot. This was the peak of a very, very bad dry season, and I imagined that Kakadu was always like this, but I found out later that the changes are absolutely dramatic.

A dentist friend of mine, Keith Bond, accompanied me and it had a major effect on him as well. We paddled around and basically worked independently. I carried my 600mm lens high into the bush, took a little light mosquito net which I strung up around me, and did a lot of pictures. It's the sort of place where you might spend a morning and afternoon and only have one encounter. You could have a lemon-breasted flycatcher land on a branch which is particularly poetically framed and you might get a lovely shot—but quite often nothing happens and you leave with only the experience. At that time in my life, accumulating large numbers of pictures wasn't an issue. It was just special to be able to sit there day after day after day and go for early morning walks and just absorb the feel of the place.

When I came back from that first trip, I was extremely depressed because the photos were dark and sinister, with blurry elements. I guess I was undergoing metamorphosis as a photographer. I thought I'd stuffed it up because at that particular point I was into sharpness and detail, but when I printed some of the images they had an amazing effect on people.

I went back to Kakadu in 1983. The whole flood plain had dried up and we were camped by deep-water billabongs. These billabongs attracted tens of thousands of birds so the place was crawling with jabirus and pelicans and egrets, and every limb and branch was occupied. The place is now an Aboriginal camp. It can't support major tourism and as I sit here in Brisbane I like the idea that Nourlangie, that special place, is largely inaccessible.

To really experience Kakadu you have to get out of your car and immerse yourself. Getting up at nine in the morning, going out in a bus and looking out a window basically gives you half a per cent of experience. You have to be up very early, and preferably on your own. Or, at most, two people together, quietly, as dawn lights come up through the grasses and trees—that's the way to experience it.

While I was working for National Parks, I was asked to do

a report on the local Aboriginal training program which had just started. It was the first in Australia where sons and daughters of traditional owners and local Aboriginal men and women were given a one-year course. Prior to that, the closest I had ever come to Aborigines was on a Townsville camp. Ian Morris was running the ranger training program and that was my first real encounter with Aboriginals. For someone who'd been brought up in Adelaide, this whole idea of visiting another culture, being involved in it, was threatening.

I've since learnt the Aboriginal way of looking at life and the earth is one we Europeans should study closely, because there is a lot of wisdom attached to Aboriginal philosophy. This whole idea of letting time pass and letting things occur rather than forcing them into happening is something we can all benefit from. I came back from that trip a different person, through the experience of being with those people.

To go bush with an Aborigine, bird-watching or photographing, is an experience in itself. What they see, what they feel, how they relate is very, very different. One day in 1983, I was up on the escarpment with a fellow called Big Bill Neidjie, of the Gagudju people, one of the traditional owners. We were at the top end of Kakadu and it was very late in the afternoon—I can remember it like it was yesterday. There was fantastic light, the flood plain was covered with birds and we were going for a walk, Big Bill, Ian and I. It was very, very hot. At the end of the day Bill came up and stood beside me, and he put a huge foot on top of mine to stop me moving away. In a very deep voice he said, 'Next time you come, there will be high rises all over this land and it will be changed. Put him in a book like he is today.' And then he said, 'I feel it with my body, my blood, all these trees, all this

country. The wind blowing. You can look . . . but feeling—
that's what makes you.'

And that's from a man who was probably about sixty, who
you would very likely drive past and think, 'He's just one of
those old Aboriginal fellows', and you wouldn't give him
credit for such depth. So this whole idea of people judging
and jeering at another culture and joining their comrades in
opinionated lunchbreak comments about Aborigines—how
do you deal with it?

What makes Kakadu disappointing to some people is their
preconceived notions about it. You see a film on TV which has
taken experts two years to make, but ninety per cent of what
they shot has been edited out. Still it blows someone's brains
out in Melbourne, Scandinavia, London or wherever, so they
get on a plane and then into a 4-wheel drive and go hundreds
of kilometres down a bitumen road. When they get there it's
all flat and maybe it's the wrong time of the year. Perhaps the
bushfires have started so it's smoky. Where are the birds, they
ask? Where is the sea eagle I saw on the film? Where is the
corroboree? It doesn't happen like that. You have to be prepared to accept that whatever happens while you are in that
place is very special. Don't have expectations, but go with the
knowledge that these things are there.

Tourists tend to move into and out of things at ninety miles
an hour. They go with a group because they feel insecure. But
if you want to experience Kakadu, go on your own. The
thought of flying to Darwin, getting off a plane, renting a car,
driving alone for four hundred kilometres, setting the alarm
clock for 3.30 am and driving out to one of the many sites
you can visit on your own would be something not many
people could contemplate.

I think Big Bill would like people to visit Kakadu. He'd want us to treat it with respect, he would like us to experience it. But the concept of 'treating with respect' has to extend further than preserving Aboriginal rock art sites. It has to apply to the way tourism is developed so that intrusion into the landscape—which is happening all around Australia—is kept to levels which do not adversely impact on indigenous people, the land or the wildlife.

When you get in an aeroplane and fly over Kakadu and look down at the infrastructure you notice it is minuscule. In relation to the enormous size of Arnhem Land, you are only talking about a few bitumen roads, turnstiles and some camping areas. It's a very minor impact. However, when you're told that uranium tailing dams in Kakadu will cause no problem, that's rubbish. The problems that arise may not be visible to the untrained eye and they may not occur for ten, fifty or two hundred years. The bottom line is that we are wreaking havoc on the environment.

I also feel some guilt because here I am publishing beautiful pictures and creating this fanciful illusion that Australia is chock-a-block full of delightful things. To some extent it's a fantasy. I've got to live with that, and where I can, I comment and assist. I guess my objective in life is to light the flame in the minds and spirits of young people so that places like Kakadu will still be there, relatively untouched, for the next generation to enjoy. **"**

A river
running through

BILL PEACH
Media personality

"The Upper Murray is very special to me—for particular personal and family reasons. In South Australia, when the Upper Murray is mentioned, they're referring to up around Renmark, which is very much the Lower Murray to me. What I mean is the first section of the river from a mountain called The Pilot, where the border of NSW begins. The major places are Tom Groggin Station—where Banjo Paterson met The Man From Snowy River—then Khancoban and the old cattle town of Corryong, then a number of small towns until you come to Hume Weir and Albury, the major city of the region.

It's not a very large area of the state—about 200 kilometres of river—but although it doesn't stretch a great distance, it rises to great heights, surrounded by the Snowy Mountains, with Kosciuszko to the north and the Bogong High Plains to the south.

I'm a fifth-generation Australian; my mother was a Sutherland and her people arrived in that region from Scotland, via Canada, well over a hundred years ago. The Sutherlands were cattle graziers and they settled on a station called Thologolong which means 'a river running through a plain'and that name describes it perfectly. It was a huge station then. Now, although I still have Sutherland relatives there, the property's shrunk to one tiny farm.

A lot of the land went under the Hume Weir in the 1930s. Thologolong was founded in 1835, not long after explorers Hume and Hovell went through. It was built like a fortress against the Dora Dora tribe—who I'm sure didn't realise they were causing such paranoia and ended up being driven off the place. It was pretty wild and remote country then and the homestead was classically long and low, with a bush-hat roof and a big veranda.

My mother was born and brought up there so when I was a child, we regularly went for holidays. We lived in Lockhart, a dry little town in the Riverina—I remember Mum rushing around, putting towels under all the doors when the dust storms came. All we had in the way of water was Brookong Creek—a chain of puddles, really—and I loved the idea of going to the river, especially the weir. When I first saw the weir, it was like an inland sea! Everything was so green and grassy and it seemed like paradise. Once when the weir was down, we saw the foundations of the original homestead—the bricks under the kitchen, the remains of an old fig tree.

We'd go on holiday by car. We had a Rugby, which was like a Model T Ford, and it was my father's pride and joy. It was a lovely old car, and it would take us a couple of hours to drive down to Albury, then another hour or so to drive up the river to Thologolong, which is right where the river starts to back up and form the Hume Weir. It was quite an expedition and we'd stay there with aunts and uncles a couple of weeks at a time, in old timber houses with possums in the roofs. All a bit hillbilly in style—but I loved that.

My grandparents had 14 children so the original station had been split up. I loved staying with my Aunt Ollie who always said she could bowl a rabbit at 50 paces with her pea rifle. She was a great shot and a champion cook who regularly won the blue ribbons for her pickles and preserves at the local show.

It was a short-sleeved summertime place—although once, much later, I was there in winter and I was shocked to discover how cold it could be—and it was right on the river, so

I'd go boating and fishing, too, which was quite a ritual. First, we'd catch yabbies for bait. We also used to get fat bardy grubs, which are similar to witchetty grubs but instead of coming from a bush, you screw them out of the ground under a certain type of red river gum. We'd fish for Murray cod and there'd always be a lot of gossip around the Dora Dora pub about who'd caught what fish. 'One time they caught an 80-pound cod,' you'd hear, 'and they couldn't get its head in a sugar bag!' There were lots of tall stories. My uncle said he caught a 10-pound cod and tethered it on a line to keep it fresh and when he came back a 60-pounder had eaten it!

There were plenty of redfin, which is a sort of English perch, but when I was a boy we'd also catch catfish and lobsters—as we used to call the big Murray River crays—and little river blackfish. Now they're all just about wiped out by the dreaded carp which were introduced, by someone who ought to be hanged, in the 1960s. They're very big and prolific and incredibly hard to kill—it's said if you throw one out, it'll crawl across a paddock and get back in the water—and they're found in every river that can be reached off the Murray and Darling system. They puddle around and destroy the clarity of the water, which kills the oxygen and makes it unlivable for other fish. And no matter how inventively you cook the carp, its taste is indescribably hideous—like something you might find at the bottom of a very old garbage bin.

We'd go swimming with ropes hanging out over the water—all those games boys play—and there were lots of horses to ride. There were endless adventures, always knowing the adults weren't keeping too close an eye. The river flows quite fast there because it's mountain country; lower down, the Murray becomes slow and wide on the plains.

My grandparents invented a new breed of cattle on Thologolong Station called the Murray Grey. It was really an accident of nature, a cross breeding between an Aberdeen Angus bull and a Shorthorn cow. The former were big, black, beefy cattle, originally from Scotland, and the latter was a roan-coloured cow. This Aberdeen Angus bull had a recessive gene, which meant it didn't continue to throw its own colour characteristics, and all the calves born became silvery grey instead of black. My grandfather thought they were freaks at first but my grandmother pleaded with him how pretty they were and so they were kept and after another generation, they were registered. They became known as the Murray Grey, which is now a recognised breed of cattle all over the world. Today there's a monument, which I unveiled about three years ago, on the Murray Valley Highway, which runs on the south side of the river, dedicated to the Sutherlands, especially my Aunt Helen, who started to scientifically breed the Murray Grey.

I still visited Thologolong when I was a teenager and even when I was at university—my mother loved to go there, it was always in her heart. Uncle Harold had a tennis court and there was a real community spirit. Dora Dora had a team and Thologolong had a team and so did Walwa, Bethanga and Tallangatta, and they'd all converge to play bush tennis and it would turn into a picnic. Even on a boiling hot Christmas Day, there'd be roast chook and hot vegetables at high noon and we'd have to play tennis afterwards and Aunt Ollie would be organising everything. She was a great character, very funny and lively, just like my mother. Real dynamo country women.

My mother died while I was living overseas but once I'd settled back in Sydney, and my father was in Albury—his roots were there, too, as his father was a blacksmith in the Albury coach factory for half a century—we resumed the Christmas holiday tradition. This time it was with my late wife, Shirley, and our children, Steve and Meredith, who were immediately converted to the delights of farm life, especially horse riding. And they'd ride around on the tractor with Uncle Harold and we'd all go down to the river to swim and fish. They became addicted to the same simple pleasures I'd loved as a boy.

Steve is now a very keen angler and he's recently been to Eucumbene, fishing. It's a good feeling to think the family traditions are being continued. My children were with me on a 1990 canoe trip I did with friends. We were looking forward to enjoying Uncle Harold's hospitality on the Victorian side of the river and the hilarity of Alf Wright's Dora Dora pub on the NSW side.

To get there, we had only to make a gentle descent of the Murray, through a beautiful valley. The river wasn't quite as gentle as we expected. Just as a long dry spell of weather is generally followed by rain, we found that tranquil reaches of the river usually concealed fast-flowing gravel rapids just around the bend.

The river would often divide into two or three channels. We were history if we didn't pick the main channel and our troubles were not over if we did. The current sometimes swerved to within a metre of the bank and there was invariably a huge weeping willow overhanging this spot. Going through a weeping willow in a canoe on a fast river is like being hurled headfirst into an eggbeater.

But the pleasure of gliding silently down the river more than compensated for a few scratches. Enormous flights of white cockatoos shrieked over our heads, brown hawks skimmed along the tree tops and kookaburras cackled from the red gums at our little convoy. The white ibis paddled in the shallows, spearing food with his long beak, and the floating lump of dark wood ahead often turned out to be a platypus.

Every night we camped on a sandy bank or an island worthy of Robinson Crusoe and cooked dinner on a campfire burning inside a sandy hollow. The sun fell and the moon rose and we saw the wondrous glory of the everlasting stars. When we retired to our tents, there was no sound but the cry of night birds and the lullaby of the river rippling over its gravelly shallows.

The landscape is calendar Australiana; Elyne Mitchell, who wrote *The Silver Brumby* and its popular sequels, lives around that way and von Guérard painted it, so evocatively, as the Victorian Alps. The skies are that intense blue you only find in Australia—the colour of the ocean with the sun on it. It's still pretty clear water in that part of the Murray, because it's fast, and there's no overdevelopment; in fact there are parks and grassed areas along the shores so in a way it's even prettier now.

Every time I go back to the Upper Murray, I feel that tie of blood, the intrinsic bond so important to our Aboriginal people. It's where you know your ancestors are buried.**"**

We belong
in the Coorong

JOHN *and* ROS MORIARTY
Designers

"Our place in the Coorong is on a peninsula called Rob's Point, known to the Aboriginal people there as Woorookurum. It's two hours south-east of Adelaide, sixteen kilometres from Meningie.

The Coorong is a seventy-five-kilometre stretch of water and on the other side of the peninsula, across from us, is Ninety Mile Beach, which starts just near the mouth of the Murray and goes right down to Robe. The Coorong is both a conservation park and a national park and it covers the mainland as well as the water. It's largely uninhabited, apart from a few fishing shacks, and we were very fortunate to get the last piece of freehold property

In the old days, the Coorong was known as 'the waterway that runs on the inside', quiet water where the fish and birds were prolific. It's still one of the foremost waterbird-breeding grounds in the Southern Hemisphere. There's a huge variety: pelicans, ducks, swans, three varieties of terns, all sorts of waders and seabirds, and we have resident wedge-tailed eagles.

The freshwater Coorong mullet is famous for eating throughout Australia. Fishermen and bird watchers love the Coorong but, because you need a four-wheel drive to get to the beach and peninsula, tourists come in dribs and drabs rather than in droves. It's a busy day if you get a couple of dozen visitors through the area. We can go and stay there and not see another human being for five days. We have two and a half hectares, plus just under a hectare which is a designated coastal protection area.

We've had the property for about four years, but John has had connections with the Coorong for a long time. There's a fishing spot about a kilometre from our place where John used to go fishing and shooting with a friend, Champ, and his wife, Elva, in the 1950s and early '60s—of course, it wasn't a protected area in those days. You could catch a lot of fish and an occasional duck, and it was easy to live off the land.

Nowadays, we enjoy the serenity and the birds, but the birdlife is not what it was in the old days. This is partly because some drains have been cut down the south-east of South Australia where the Coorong was automatically flushed after big rains, and that doesn't happen any more. The local Aborigines, the Ngarrindje people, particularly Robert Day and Tom and George Trevorrow, want it changed back to the old system and are trying to persuade the River Murray-Darling Basin Authority to reinstate the drainage system so the Coorong can be brought back to what it was.

Despite being a lovely, peaceful place, the Coorong has tempestuous moods, especially its strong winds. Our place was built with all those weather aspects in mind. It can range from hot, quiet, still days to bitterly cold periods with fierce winds that whip across the southern part of Australia. We're on an exposed headland, with 270-degree views over water. We chose that position for its solitude and the building's feeling of snugness from the storms. The house is angled not only toward the view but to the sun; it's very energy-efficient. We live there in splendid isolation. Our brief to the architect was to build a shelter that didn't intrude upon or alienate the site but was nevertheless distinctive. We had three priorities: a view of the moon on the water from the bedroom, getting the central fireplace right, and, to enjoy the elements, we wanted an indoor-outdoor place.

The sunsets, in particular, are magnificent. One Christmas, the sky was on fire. It had been breathlessly still and silver-grey as the sun went down. And the water looked like polished silver, too, and the pelicans were skimming along, and there were perfect mirror images of them in the water. And then at about 11 pm, the storm hit South Australia and you could see it coming for kilometres. Until that moment, everything had been dead calm. Then the sky was split with lightning, the thunder came, and pounding rain lashed the house for hours.

For both of us, there's a real feeling of spirituality in the Coorong. Almost every time we are there, something quite extraordinary happens, whether it's a yellow orb of a moon, too enormous to be true, or thousands of pelicans drifting up off the cliff with the wind currents. Last year, we saw dolphins in the Coorong, but no one's ever, ever seen dolphins there. They were bronze-black, leaping next to our sailing cat. Very eerie and supernatural. It was a small pod—probably just one family—and we saw them for just two or three minutes.

On the surf beach, you can get stingrays gobbling cockles as the waves thunder in—those huge stingrays that are five or six feet across. They're half out of the water, with the cockles, reeling back, and they go out with the waves and come back. Ros was walking along in knee-deep water, and this thing went around one side of her and back, as the wave came in; she didn't realise it was there until I pointed it out. The cockles we collect are sweet and big; Ros cooks them in a green curry—just magnificent.

We draw inspiration for our designs from this landscape and its colours, both directly and indirectly. The sand there is blinding white and the contrast of the brilliant blue sky with the Sahara-like dunes, the hot sun beating down, that's a magical combination. We came up with one recent collection that was absolutely based on Coorong coastal colours. It features stylised images of shells and birds, using textures of bush sponges and grasses. We tried to capture the light of the Coorong and the clarity of its colours, the jades and turquoises of the sea, the creams of neutral stones, the oranges of sunset. The stars, for example, are astonishingly bright. We don't need a torch to go out at night: the sky's ablaze.

It's a comforting feeling—like returning to the cradle—to drive to the Coorong after a very stressful week. The tension just falls away. Our three children love doing all those beachy things we did as kids—looking for crabs, beachcombing, getting up to mischief in the water, kayaking, sailing the cat, canoeing. There are a lot of bedrooms and bathrooms at our place so we can have large gatherings with three or four families, tons of kids. Most of these have been really memorable, maybe because of a fantastic meal or playing board-games until late at night—almost like a holiday camp! And the way the kitchen is constructed, you can have five or six people in there, pouring a glass of wine and preparing something to eat, always with loads of laughter. And great music. Often jazz.

The place seems to have a magnetic attraction for everyone who goes there. For instance, some friends who went back to Germany sent a note and instead of enquiring how we were, they asked, 'How's the Coorong?' The movie *Storm Boy* was made on the same stretch of water, a little further along, and more of Colin Thiele's books are based there, so some of the images, especially the pelicans, are familiar to many Australians.

Camp Coorong, an ecotourism operation about three or four kilometres away from our place, is thriving and kids are being taught about the Aboriginal culture and the environment by Ngarrindjeri people. We've had large contingents of Japanese visit us, so they can experience the landscapes which have influenced our collections. The Japanese and the Germans, in particular, appreciate our very strong sense of place. People who meditate appreciate the Coorong, too—for its solitude, its spirituality and its unspoilt beauty.

The Coorong really is a place of magic moments. Pelicans silhouetted against the moon, wild storms, cooking cockles collected on the beach. It is a haven. **,,**

Mellow brick
road

RICHARD NEVILLE
Writer and Commentator

"What drew me to the wilderness was partly nostalgia, because when I was a teenager my mother bought a weekender at Mount Victoria, the highest point in the Blue Mountains. It was a quaint village back then, incredibly boring in a way, but ringed with secretive, overgrown bush tracks with names like Fairies Glen and Bushranger's Cave. It was the first time I had seen any nature apart from the coastline.

Then I disappeared to London and forgot all about it, holed up in a basement making metaphorical molotov cocktails. When I returned to Australia in the 1970s, the impact of the mountains was profound.

One afternoon I went for a stroll down a dull-sounding track, Porter's Pass, and as it progressed through ferny glens, a waterfall, a swirl of rockpools, and dropped down a cliff-carved stairway, I realised I was walking in a work of art. Ever unfolding. Who was this person called Porter? I felt an overwhelming identification with, not the Aboriginal element at all, but these timid British solicitors and surveyors who had come out here and hewed a trail of ecstasy out of ironstone. It took incredible skill, requiring aesthetic judgement and geological wisdom, so I guess it just drew me in.

A few minutes from the back door of our home, you can descend into the Grose Valley—no cars, no shops—and walk along a trail for days; though I usually come up at Govetts Leap. Others bone up on the walks in greater detail than me; I'm a bit of a dilettante. I do love them, but I don't pore over contour maps and memorise each gully. Some of my relatives go off with ropes and packs and Lilos, and white-water the canyons. It's a bit of a fad. Each weekend the cliffs are covered with abseilers, rock climbers and rescue helicopters. Come Monday, and all is serene—apart from the black cockatoos.

Living in the Blue Mountains, you don't have to be reminded of starry nights. You don't have to look up the calendar to see if there's a full moon. When there's a storm over Sydney, you don't have to watch it on the news. You don't have to go to an Oxygen Bar to breathe exquisite air. You're close to primal forces, and ultimately, if this is a good thing or a bad thing, I don't know, but it's a turbulent place to live. Elemental.

Some people argue that you shouldn't live in power spots, that it's psychically overwhelming. Earlier this year, as we were loading the car for our summer holidays, the lightning struck three times, scorching our phone, our fax, our computer. It happens often, even melting the surge busters. Kangaroos and possums enjoy the taste of a phone cable; bushfires threaten every few years. It keeps you on your toes.

It's a unique environment for kids. There are disadvantages, as they don't get so streetwise, or so hip to the latest video games. Friends recently came out from the States with a son the same age as my daughter. He sat down at the piano and played a burst of Beethoven, and I could see my daughter becoming overawed, a little ill-at-ease. Then we went on a bushwalk, and my daughter was swinging from trees and dangling off cliffs, and this little boy shrank into his own kind of phobia, so it was a relief to see how things balance out.

And they do. Kids can live out their fantasies in a world before virtual reality. I've got a nine-year-old nephew at Mount Victoria who paints himself up as an Aboriginal and can name every species of bird, plant and butterfly. I recently took him to Australia's Wonderland, the theme park, and all he cared about was that he spotted a blue-crested honeyeater.

Politics? I used to march against the war in Vietnam, and now I'm marching against McDonalds. What does this mean? Maybe the McDonaldisation of the world is the final victory of those very same forces that tried to colonise Vietnam. This is not an attack on people eating hamburgers, and I know a lot of kids wouldn't have a job if it weren't for fast food. Born free, we are everywhere in franchise chains.

But I guess my philosophy is one of enclave areas. If we're going to give private enterprise a free rein, then when a place seems a bit special, and I don't mean special only for the rich—whether it's Broome, Bermagui, Byron Bay or the Blue Mountains—I think it's worth fighting to keep it as an enclave, because in the future they'll be much more valuable spiritually and even commercially than as part of the homogenised mainstream.

For some reason, 99 per cent of Australians are keen to make everywhere like everywhere else. It's a national obsession to turn Coffs Harbour into Parramatta Road. It must reassure people. My own inclination is the other way around. So I fight for the pockets of complexity, for spaces to breed alternatives, in terms of lifestyle and imagination. Some experiments might be whacky and crazy and dead ends, others could help re-invent the future.

The mountains are a cultural flashpoint. While there's a high degree of poverty here, lots of struggling single parents, welfare recipients making the best of cheap rents, many new settlers come for positive reasons—the spectacular chasms, plus you can park easily, chat to the postmistress, watch the leaves change colour, sit by a wood fire. It's a slower pace than the city. Writers, artists and musicians are moving up, the place is crawling with Buddhists, rock climbers, and ultra-serious chefs. There's a growth industry in ashrams and retreat centres. Two of the best bakeries in the country—Quinton's at Leura and the Blackheath Patisserie—have enhanced mountain breakfasts, afternoon teas, and desserts. The Varuna Writers' Centre at Katoomba is flourishing. Plenty of people garden, paint, write poetry, practise yoga, play heavy metal guitar. But jobs are short, so tourism is seen as a godsend.

At the moment we're bringing in as many planes as possible, whacking the punters into expensive hotels, into air-conditioned buses, driving them to lookouts, saying gee whiz, taking them shopping and putting them back on the plane. This is a pretty crass, 1950s-style, industrial revolution approach. Factory fodder, battery hens. What about the inner journey? There are unemployed and under-utilised people with skills in massage, meditation, bushwalking, abseiling. Let's get tourists out of the buses and into the gorges. I don't care whether it's Mum, Dad and the kids or burnt-out execs from the Asian 'Tigers' that yearn to be psychically retooled.

The first tourists were pilgrims . . . on their way to sacred sites. There's even an echo of this sense of pilgrimage the way we stare at the Three Sisters. Now the sacred site is a shopping mall, and the litany of tourism includes frequent flier points, fast food, air-conditioned buses. Take the road to my house—sure, it's dirt, and the car slides round, and yes, it messes the duco. The buses demand kerbs and guttering, which changes everything. Less trees, birds and kangaroos; more noise. It's a short-term mentality about tourism, which is bums on seats. Actually, everything is bums on seats, these days.

Twenty years from now, people will look back on this era of anal economics as a bizarre quirk, an aberration, a failure of imagination. Some Europeans come here and are frightened by the untrammelled wilderness. All these trees look the same, the writer Shiva Naipaul told me, it's so dreary: there are no ancient gardens, no milky statues. His idea of wilderness was classic Arcadia: vineyards, cherubs, gambolling Pan. Our wilderness was apparently horrible—barren and full of serpents.

Fortunately for me, this place in the heart is two hours from the city and you can plug into its energy. At night, all the city lights come up; by day, I see the golden tower of Centrepoint. I love that, too. The beat of the city is palpable, the Emerald City glitters. On an impulse, you can hop on a train and lunch in Chinatown.

Bushwalks are a good place to go on a first date. A bottle of wine, a loaf of bread, a tin of sardines and she beside you in the wilderness. It's romantic, building up a campfire. You can get each other's measure on a bushwalk, it's where I courted my wife. So naturally we got married at Govetts Leap. Of course they pretend that Govett was a bushranger who jumped off the escarpment, guns blazing, and there's a statue to prove it. Actually Govett was a government surveyor and 'leap' is a Scottish word for gorge.

Let's not get sentimental about the weather in the mountains, it's often vile. It can be misty for months, it can be incredibly hot with squadrons of flying sheep, the national bird, also known as blowflies. It can be hideous. And sometimes when I go to a cute little fishing village like Bermagui [on the NSW south coast], I think, why am I living in the mountains when I could be eating fresh fish and swimming every day? Yes, you do miss the ocean.

And that's not all you miss. You can love the mountains and still pine for a spring in Manhattan. In fact, one of the first columns that my wife, Julie, wrote for *HQ* magazine was about this schizophrenia. You always carry the shadow, the reflection of the road not taken. In my early years I lived an external life. Prematurely publicised, exuding an unhealthy trail of press clippings. Maybe moving here was an unconscious recognition of a need to go a bit internal, and for that you do need a certain amount of space and tranquillity. I'm not saying I plotted all this out, but it was probably an unconscious adjunct to the motivation to move here.

Not that you prowl the cliffs every day—although I'll tell you what, the walks at night, when you're in the middle of a chapter: amazing. So I can see why writers were drawn to the cliffs.

I've just returned from Bangkok. The hotels are thrusting ever upwards, every building has a crane on it, the traffic is gridlocked, they've filled in all the canals, the policemen wear smog masks and you can barely see across the street. And what's the latest hot product? Comfort 100. You can guess its use. A bedpan for drivers stuck on a freeway!

That's completely horrific, and yet I loved my spell in Bangkok, sort of *Bladerunner* meets *Johnny Mnemonic*. On the verge of the inferno. There is something stimulating about the abyss. I don't want to convey the impression that one must retreat from the metropolis, sit in the mountains and vegetate. I try to use this place for renewal, to process some inner material, but also to stay in touch with other parts of the world.

I guess the best journalism, or at least my favourite kind of journalism, is the quirky columns by fabulous writers—an art form that can transcend journalism, and can be personal, wry and illuminating, dating back to James Thurber and beyond. So now I can fire up a modem and pick over the ideas in interactive magazines like *Salon* and the *Utne Reader* which are trying to harness the creative potential of the Internet as opposed to worshipping its technology. What a change from the soapstar wank mags put out by the moguls. Of course I do like to have a conversation with somebody brighter than myself, and there are many people who fit into that category, perhaps too many, and they're only a few seconds away in cyberspace. So that has added another dimension to living on a mountain.

There's a terrific group of people up here, and the café society is just starting to get its act together. The Blue Mountains has been slow in finding its social centre—partly because so many of us are in our home offices, working round the clock in pyjamas. Also, the geography has been hostile— just a suburban strip along a ridge connected by the most dangerous highway in Australia. Every mile or so you notice a little wooden cross, a bunch of dying flowers tied to it. We know all too well what that means. Basically, once a week a semi overturns, or rams a Commodore, and we all go on pretending it's a fluke, but it's part of the commuter lifestyle. We have to get the semi-trailers off our highway and use the goods trains; perhaps nothing will be done until a whole tourist busload is flattened under a semi.

Having travelled extensively, I know just how lucky I am to be able to live inside a natural wilderness populated by the most rare and exquisite species of plants and animals. It's a miracle. We've found a spotted eastern quoll eating the scraps in the kitchen, and even though the tiger snake in the bedroom was a bit off-putting, it was another experience for the kids to pass on to their grandchildren. **99**

In a Sydney state of mind

MARELE DAY
Writer

"I grew up in an archetypal Sydney suburb. We lived on the main road, which was built during the Second World War, about the same time as the Burma Road, and was known back then as the New Burma Road, and when my family moved there, it was ripe for development. Eastlakes Golf Course is nearby and it was a huge source of adventure when I was a kid. It was like being in the country, hiding in the bushes, finding golf balls, pretending we were cowboys and indians.

Before the sewer was put in, it seemed all very exciting when the dunny man came. He was like the bogey man, with black clothes and this image of darkness. When trenches for the sewer were being dug, all the back fences had to be pulled down and we kids could just move from place to place. That brought a real sense of community but I found the suburb itself very sterile—it wasn't until I'd travelled and returned to live in the inner city that I recognised Sydney as really being my place.

Now the part of Sydney with which I feel the most affinity is the inner west. I like the architecture, its character, the degree of dilapidation—although given the amount of gentrification, that's probably not the right word. In the real suburbs, you could never be anonymous, your neighbours would always know what you were doing. The anonymity of the inner west is to do with mobility and the shift in population, too. Prior to the 1960s, people lived in the inner city for generations: my grandmother, for example, died next door to the house in which she was born, in Alexandria. That process of staying put was quite characteristic of the working class in the inner city.

My childhood ambition was to be a teacher, but also to travel. The atlas was the book I pored over when I was supposed to be doing my homework. I planned journeys that included names which sang with allure and colour—dry, sandy Samarkand, sun-drenched Madrid. Vladivostok had the kick of chilled vodka, red-and-green Tierra del Fuego was a pleasure trip for the tongue. When I was 11, my cousin went 'overseas' on the *Fairsky*. The ship was huge—bigger than a block of flats. Circular Quay was a mass of streamers, high hopes, nervousness, excited chatter and sensible parental advice. We found our way to the cramped, stuffy cabin on D Deck that my cousin was sharing with three other girls. Heaven. Adventures, midnight snacks, giggling in the dorms and no parents. A floating boarding school.

Ten years later, I found myself in the place of my dreams— a cramped, stuffy cabin on the *Fairsky*. We disembarked in Lisbon on a cold, grey February morning. I distinctly remember standing on the dock with a suitcase full of evening dresses and saying to my friend, 'What do we do now?'

We found a pension. We didn't speak Portuguese and they didn't speak English, but it soon became obvious that the pension wanted our passports. We shook our heads fiercely. No way. Our parents had told us never to let our passports out of our sight: 'Even when you're swimming, wear it in a plastic bag around your waist.'

Eventually the police had to come to explain that in Portugal it was customary for the pension to keep guests' passports for the duration of their stay. We looked at each other and did what we had to do. The first day overseas and here we were relinquishing our passports. All the other parental advice quickly followed suit. We were on our way.

I always wanted the experience of living in a different place, rather than the nomadism of travelling. It's been said you either get a real appreciation of a place in the first two days, otherwise you have to be there for 20 years. I ended up spending two years in Ireland, in County Cork. I had a friend who was living there who suggested I come over for a look, as the Irish say. So I went over for a look and ended up staying two years. I don't have any Irish heritage, but it was another place that felt like home. When I first arrived in the village, on this remote island, I was waiting for my friend to meet me so I went into the pub and as soon as I opened my mouth, they knew I was Australian. The guy behind the bar asked, 'How's the Coogee Bay Hotel going?' He'd worked in Sydney for 10 years!

I recognised the look of the countryside from the *Girl's Own Annuals* of my youth: the little flowers in the hedgerows, a whimsical landscape very different to the Australian bush with its dryness and danger. Our bush never seems to me a friendly place for Europeans. All those snakes and spiders and the need to keep your shoes on.

Ireland is like an emotional second home to me, I feel great affinity with the place. And the people—they have poetry in their soul. You go to a pub and they'll be reciting verses or quoting James Joyce; they really have the gift of the gab. When I left Ireland, it was with great regret, knowing that nothing would ever be the same.

In Sydney, I feel as if I'm holding the fort because five generations of my family have lived here and I'm the only one left. My parents have opted out of 'the Big Smoke' and retired to the country but I'm afraid I would just veg out, look at the scenery and do nothing. Perhaps it's silly, but I feel a responsibility to stay.

What I discovered about Sydney when I started writing the Claudia Valentine books was what you see is not always what you get. There is always a beautiful facade but underneath there's a lot of refuse; the city was built on a garbage tip, really. I remember the first moment I felt like writing about Sydney—it was when I came back from Ireland. I was in the Botanic Gardens, with that amazing view of the harbour which I think Sydneysiders get very blasé about. You don't become aware of it until you've been away. I thought I'd like to put this city on the map, to provide an image for that word, Sydney. If we say Los Angeles or New York, everybody has an image of those places and I wondered what Sydney actually means.

To me, it's blue and grey, a place that's in love with itself. I think the water is a great image for Sydney because it has discernible moods, it's always moving. Surface is a word I'd use to describe Sydney—sparkling, reflective. Paris is yellow, it has a certain glow, and London is red—I suppose it's the buses. As I stood in the Botanic Gardens looking at the harbour, I realised that was the view people had on migrant ships and even if all they had was one little cardboard suitcase, they were arriving in what looked like Utopia.

But it must have been terrible in Sydney when the colony began: starvation, high mortality, disease. It might be simplistic to say the origins have an indelible mark on the descendants of a place but think of the Puritan element in America, fighting all the time, a libertarian thread. In Sydney, what you get is beauty mingled with the convict streak and it may have something to do with the water. Certainly for a writer, I have this image of how it shifts and moves all the time—things are very shallow rooted in Sydney as opposed to, say, Melbourne, which is staunch, solid, conservative, intent on keeping the surface the same as the roots.

Sydney's shallowness is probably to do with the climate, as well; it's warmer than Melbourne and if you think about tropical vegetation, it's all shallow rooted, the lushness is on the surface and there is hardly any nourishment underneath. In Claudia Valentine's terms, you get sleaze beneath this beautiful facade. You get corruptness or rot at the heart of things—and that's another tropical image, a beautiful flower which can be fetid at its centre. Melbourne has better bookshops and restaurants, probably, but they are both indoor pursuits. Sydney is racy, trashy and hedonistic but I love every minute of it. I haven't settled here because it's like that but I accept the way it is.

But there are things about Sydney I don't like. There's a great deal of urban ugliness—just take a trip along Parramatta Road and look at those awful car yards. When I first returned, I realised there wasn't a lot of civic pride and people didn't seem to appreciate public spaces or views. In fact, the view is a very contemporary concept for Sydneysiders and we pay a lot for it. David Williamson has commented that everybody in Sydney is here for the view and even if you don't live with it outside your door, you come into the city to see it. Melburnians aren't as interested in views—after all, where *are* their views?

I think the Asianisation of Sydney is very exciting, particularly in terms of food. It's cheaper to go to Cabramatta than Hong Kong and you get all that variety and atmosphere. Most people do talk about migrant influences in terms of food rather than a world view or philosophy or thousands of years of culture which might come from those places. But in a new culture, you are not forced to stay within a framework, you can be like a bowerbird and take what you like.

During the course of research for Claudia Valentine, I've discovered that Sydney is a series of little villages, often like concentric circles, some overlapping. Cabramatta is the most obvious example. It's amazing how quickly that happened. In the 1950s it was fibro houses, the square Australian suburban shape, and now it's got exotic curly edges. You can walk around Cabramatta all afternoon and see only five non-Asian faces. Then there's Strathfield, which is rather Indian and, although it's always possible these comfort zones can breed ghettos, it's balanced by that notion of space and an openness. I don't think you can get away from the physicality of the landscape and the effect it has on Sydneysiders.

I'm trying to understand the views of Pauline Hanson's followers. Are they threatened because we have always felt alien in our surroundings? There has always been the fear of the Yellow Peril, that Asians were going to come and get us, that this was the best country in the world and everyone wanted to live here. They don't! That's the irony. I think the British still own more of Australia than anyone.

I'd like Claudia Valentine to go on another adventure, possibly in a different city. I really wanted to write about Sydney, with the city as a real character and I think the human characters in the book are the sort this city produces: flexible, changing, willing to take risks, laconic sense of humour, with a kind of built-in bullshit meter. But I think I have come to the conclusion of the cycle with Claudia—maybe not the end of her as a character altogether. *The Disappearances of Madalena*

Grimaldi solved the ongoing mystery of her father and that brought some resolution.

Claudia wouldn't know another city as well as Sydney so the perspective would be different. She's allowed to make critical comments about Sydney because we know that's where she lives. I don't want her to be a whinger making comments as she would at home, but I think she's a good vehicle to be able to debunk the myths of other places—like Paris always has the best food in the world, and so on. But the Claudia we know now is a tour guide for Sydney—she loves it and she's good at it.

There are fictional places that are important to me as well—for example, the island monastery in my new novel *Lambs of God*. It is a high, windy island covered in gorse and other vegetation typical of windswept places. Inside the monastery walls, it is gentler: green grass dotted with sheep. The island exists only in the imagination, yet while writing the book, I was there, I could see it and feel it. **"**

Chapter 3

LOVE AT FIRST SIGHT

Falling head over heels
for an unfamiliar place

Hooray for Bollywood

SUSAN KUROSAWA
Writer

"India affects me like nowhere else. It startles and seduces in equal degrees. Before my first visit, in the early 1980s, I read a description that being in India was like lying, relaxed and happy, in a warm scented bath and then every so often an electric shock would come charging through the water. At the time, I wasn't sure what that meant, but after 10 visits and the full gamut of emotions—I have boxed a troublesome tour guide about the ears with my guidebook and wept with sheer delight at the absurdity of camel races during the Pushkar Fair—I now know you can never afford to be complacent when dealing with Mother India.

On my most recent trip, I fulfilled another step in what seems to be my 'Indianisation'. Astrologers in Agra and Madras have told me I was Indian in my last life, and although I half-believe they tell every Indiophile client the same thing—and you've always been a bejewelled maharani and never the goat-herder's third wife—I often have such strong *deja-vu* in India, that I wonder if they could be right. So, with a red *bindi* spot on my forehead and some lavish backcombing, I managed to secure a walk-on part in an Indian movie— one of those pot-boilers starring veiled virgins with heaving bosoms and heroes in wide suits who can shoot around corners.

Ever since I attended my first Hindi song-and-dance epic, at the Coronation Talkies cinema in Ooty, I've loved the jangly music, the preposterous plots, the way the hero always gets his girl—but not before he's been sorely tempted by a Bad Woman with too much eyeliner—and the coy love scenes where the cameras cut to bluebirds of happiness and gushing fountains every time there's a suggestion of a kiss.

In a land of such widespread poverty, bleak movies are hardly going to be drawcards, so huge crowds turn up to the love hits for a belt of escapism. There are standing-room-only sections where young boys take it in turns to climb on each other's shoulders to see the screen. And the movies are long, sometimes three or four hours—it's all about value for money. They say there are around 12,000 cinemas across India, many in the poorest of rural areas, where filmgoers arrive, like pilgrims to a shrine, after walking for hours.

I spent several days at Film City on the outskirts of Bombay—or Mumbai, I should say, if we are to use its new politically correct name—which is the headquarters of Bollywood, a multi-million-dollar industry which churns out the world's highest quota of movies. Quantity, not quality, is the key, and the studios work around the clock in assembly-line fashion. It's only recently that a ceiling was imposed on how many films a star can be making at one time; it's rumoured that the record is 27 features for one leading heart-throb who was so in demand he had to smooth his moustache, adjust his sabre and lurch from one mystifying script to the next.

I was cast as the third bar girl in a nightclub scene which meant the director kept yelling for 'B3' to pout harder and pour more drinks. This title made me feel like a new addition to the Bananas in Pyjamas team, something which I tried to explain to the wardrobe mistress as she constantly readjusted my cleavage and called for more mascara. Sick of my gibbering, she finally told me that Indian people rarely slept with their bananas and, if I knew anything about Bollywood, I would realise that all the big starlets 'were sleeping totally without any form of pyjamas whatsoever'.

The top movie stars in India are treated like royalty. When

the 1980s maharajah of the movies, Amitabh Bachchan, was accidentally shot during a fight scene and lay in hospital with severe stomach injuries, the nation held mass prayer meetings for his recovery and the then prime minister flew to his bedside. TV programs were interrupted with news flashes on the state of his appetite and the frequency of his bowel movements. In a way, it's a shame he recovered—all India had been looking forward to a public holiday and the most notable funeral since Mahatma Gandhi's.

Mother India is not for everyone, particularly those travellers with squeamish stomachs who couldn't tolerate squalor and dirt, lepers and beggars. But those of us who love India— who rejoice in her spirituality and the will of her people to survive—embrace her, warts, triplicate forms, terrible toilets and all.

India's star attraction is her people. Both her greatest asset and her most intolerable burden, they involve you, the hapless tourist, on a journey of discovery in which, from my experience, you find out as much about yourself as this bizarre place you are visiting. I have learnt so much about my levels of tolerance and powers of endurance and compassion in India, that I feel compelled to return again and again. It's almost as if I can't come to terms with who I really am unless I am there, being tested and almost swallowed whole by the sheer complexity and vigour of the place.

The images career and collide in my mind. There was the boatman who tried to sell me a block of hashish as big as a housebrick as he propelled me across Srinagar's Lake Dal in a shikara boat with ancient velvet curtains and a hand-painted sign announcing: Full Spring Seating. How to forget the young chap who played jaunty tunes on his flute as I swayed up to Jaipur's glorious Amber Fort atop a decorated elephant. He told me I looked like Elizabeth Taylor and when I didn't tip enough, he cleverly added, 'But when she was young and beautiful in *Butterfield 8*.' Don't bother looking for him if you go to the Amber Fort. I suspect he's banked my tip and moved to the Caribbean!

Then there was the devilishly moustachioed Sikh in a Bombay bazaar who sniffily regarded me when I asked directions to a toilet and announced, 'Please, Madam, all India is a toilet.' And the village women gathered around a well in the Rajasthan desert with their popsicle-pink saris and flashing gold jewellery who shared their precious water with me and shyly prodded my shoulder-pads, giggling helplessly at such Western artifice. In tropical Cochin, in the prosperous west-coast state of Kerala, my travelling companion, Christine McCabe, and I sat on our hotel balcony sipping 'oozing beauties'—Kampa Cola and ice cream from a special 'mocktail' list—and had a feeling we were being watched. We looked over the balcony and could see no one about. A sudden noise above made us glance up and then we found our audience: two off-duty waiters, grinning ear-to-ear, dangling upside down like bats from the upstairs balcony rail, thoroughly enjoying their view of the two mad memsahibs and their foamy drinks.

The gaggle of little girls in the precincts of the Taj Mahal at Agra who twittered with delight when I let them play with my lipstick. I sat under a shady tree while they painted their faces and never did get around to looking inside India's most famous monument. Mother India can always find ways to make you dally.

Then there was the earnest young man in the marketplace

at Simla, the old summer capital of the Raj, who solemnly offered to exchange an exquisite moonstone bracelet for my Nike runners. The shoes were covered with half the Himalaya and smelt like ripe cheese but he wanted a pair of brand-name running shoes so badly he was almost bursting. So we came to a compromise: he took the shoes and his cousin arrived with a pair of sandals for me. Plus a pair of woolly red socks as it was mid-winter. I wore those sandals all over India and had my bright red toes polished by over-eager shoeshine boys from one end of the country to the other.

India does funny things to my sense of decorum. In Mysore's Lalitha Mahal palace-hotel dining room—a birth-day-cake-blue eating area the size of an aircraft hangar—I waited an hour to be served. The place was empty and I'd been seated right in the middle at a table as far as possible from the kitchen and the view. Finally, I set alight my menu using a box of matches thoughtfully provided on the table, perhaps for just such a purpose. I held the menu aloft like a distress signal as a waiter sprinted toward me. 'Vegetable curry, extra hot,' I beamed, as he poured a jug of iced water over me.

India is an endurance test. First rule of survival is that there's absolutely no point trying to buck the system. This is a country where bureaucracy of the closely printed triplicate form and important rubber stamp variety has been perfected as an art form. Lone women travellers, in particular, would do well to maintain a madonna calm. For starters, you have to get used to being suspiciously quizzed by everyone from hotel managers to hawkers on the whereabouts of your husband and babies.

To cope in this land of sleeping dogs and status quo, one

capitulates. Even when bargaining, you're likely to wind up as the novelty in the cultural cracker. After ruthlessly haggling with a hawker in Goa to bring down the price of a box of pop-up Julie's Jumbo Tissues to ten rupees, I ripped open the coarse wrapper to discover the maximum retail price printed as six rupees. And of course Julie had the final word as she refused to pop up a single one and I had to destroy the box to wipe my nose.

It's hard to choose a favourite spot in India but I'm very fond of Udaipur in the desert state of Rajasthan. It's a sizeable city on a lake ringed with cool green hills—it looks like a mirage after you've been travelling for days aboard a camel in the rolling sands. In the middle of Lake Pichola sits the Lake Palace Hotel, a low white building which appears, from a distance, on a calm day, like an embellished wedding cake sitting on a huge silver-blue platter. Built over a 30-year period in the 17th century in what I call 'the confectionery school of architecture', this hotel used to be one of the many homes of the Maharana of Udaipur. Like dozens of regal residences, it was converted to accommodation after Independence in 1947. There's marble by the mile, staff dressed in the traditional firecracker-red turbans and cummerbunds of the one-time palace staff, and the top suites twinkle with mirrored mosaic tiles.

Rajasthan has many other palace-hotels, all affordable and offering oases of opulence, boltholes where you can gather your resources before re-entering the fray. In Jodhpur, for instance, the Umaid Bhawan Palace is a grand biscuity-coloured sandstone building that before its conversion to a hotel was touted to be the world's largest private residence. It's in Art Deco style—on steroids, considering the scale—

and has an indoor swimming pool, musical crystal fountain and guestrooms so vast and far flung that room service really needs to be delivered by couriers, not waiters.

The erstwhile Maharajah of Jodhpur is still in residence in an upstairs apartment; he potters about in his slippers and takes constitutionals around the vast gardens. I tried to organise an interview with him one morning but was told he was far too busy to meet the press—he had to wind his clock collection.

Not all my India experiences have been pleasant. In late-1992, Christine and I had a ridiculous time aboard a 'luxury' train for a week. It was promoted as the ultimate five-star experience and despite making brave little jokes about being 'upwardly mughal' as we chugged along in our tiny compartment, we spent the entire week vomiting and hiding from our fellow passengers—Swiss Germans who kept complaining that India was dirty. We decided that was a bit like being surprised to find snow at the South Pole.

We couldn't work out why we were so sick: we ate sparingly and drank only bottled water. It wasn't until we spotted our cabin attendant refilling the plastic 'mineral water' bottles from a tap on a railway platform that we realised we'd been drinking liquid dysentery.

Still recovering from our doses of subcontinental railway traveller's stomach, we headed for Calcutta. We were cross with India, as one tends to get, despite every good intention of stoicism. It was the time of the burning of a disputed mosque at Ayodhya and religious unrest was crackling through the country, especially in West Bengal, a fact Indian Airlines had not thought to tell us as we boarded a plane from Delhi for riot-torn Calcutta.

A curfew on the city was imposed minutes after our taxi swept around the circular drive of our hotel and its handsome wrought-iron gates clanked shut behind us. They were to stay firmly closed for the next three days as the City of Joy quietly simmered, headlines screeched 'Shoot-at-sight order in Calcutta' and streets in this city of 11 million stood astonishingly empty, save for a few hours of breakneck traffic each midday as the curfew was lifted and little black auto-rickshaws scuttled about like fleeing cockroaches.

My sightseeing of Calcutta was achieved via coffee-table books provided by the management. Staff slept in hotel quarters and tried their best to jolly along guests by providing free passes to the health club—'sorry, closed until further notice'—and organising treasure hunts by the pool. I didn't participate, suspecting the prize was probably a city tour.

We eventually escaped one steamy afternoon when the curfew was lifted long enough for a hotel car to transport us to the airport. Naturally, it broke down and we had to pay a passing taxi-driver's family food bill for a year to get to the fabulously named Dum Dum Airport. We felt only a moment's guilt as he turfed out his previous and less desperate passengers and left them stranded by the side of the road.

It's best I don't go into details of how we actually got ourselves onto an overbooked flight, but it did involve kicking, biting and a fistful of American dollars. Once on board, we cursed India black and blue. But, it was a few days before Christmas and as we pondered spending the holiday season in safe and orderly Sydney where the planes and trains run on schedule and dysentery is the stuff of exotic research, we felt unutterably depressed and wondered if we pooled our greenbacks and bribed the captain, perhaps he'd fly us back. **"**

Frontiers of heaven

CHRISTINE GEE
Businesswoman

"My father, Allan Gee, raised me with the philosophy of 'never being frightened to live or frightened to die'. He was a survivor of HMAS *Perth* and spent three and a half years on an unwanted trip on the Burma railway as a Japanese prisoner-of-war. Prior to being captured, Dad had been around the world five times and had visited such exotic places as Durban and Jamaica and attended the 1939 World's Fair in New York. So I was raised by a passionate traveller with a relish for exploring.

My love affair with the Himalaya began in the Victorian country town of Beechworth's primary school when I was just nine. My teacher, Mr Cruickshank, was pointing to Mount Everest on a map and although distracted by the dried egg splattered across his green hand-knitted jumper, I remember very clearly the thrall of seeing that small dot.

But I wasn't to make contact with Everest, or Nepal, again until 1975, after completing my degree at the Australian National University in Canberra. I was on the lookout for student accommodation and in response to a newspaper ad, I knocked on the door of a house in the Canberra suburb of Lyneham. It was opened by a tall Welshman called Goronwy Price. We spent most of the evening talking about Nepal, as Goronwy had only recently returned from a trek to Everest and he had the expression of someone who'd just found religion.

I was captivated by his stories of the Himalaya and moved into the house without further ado, a decision which was to change my life. In the process, I ended up co-owning a trekking company and being consumed by a passion for Nepal for the next 14 years.

It began with my first trek to the Himalaya, an undertaking nothing short of a fairytale come to larger-than-life fruition. The magic began as soon as I landed at Kathmandu Airport and Goronwy was there to greet me, weighed down with garlands of marigolds.

We set out for Pokhara which nestles by a very beautiful lake and it was there that we made camp. Goronwy told me that in the morning I was in for a surprise I would never forget. At dawn, when I popped my head outside the tent, I was greeted with the most beautiful sight I have ever seen: marshmallow tufts of peaks rising up across the Western Himalaya in an endless march along the horizon. I felt I had left the earth.

We planned to trek in the Annapurna region of West Nepal, and I must say that prior to setting out, my notion of walking in the mountains was a very romantic one indeed. Trekking, as I soon discovered, is quite hard work at times, with no promise of a shower or bath for at least two or three weeks. But after the first few days, you start to feel fitter and the scenery proves a constant source of inspiration. Life becomes very simple when you're trekking and that's why I love it so much. The constant ringing of phones, roar of traffic and intermittent fire and car alarms are replaced by the sounds of silence, children at play and a lone yak herder singing as he struggles with his herd. The only worries you have are whether or not to eat another chapatti and how far it is to the next tea stop.

While the mountains are Nepal's number one drawcard, the most enduring memory, for me, remains the warmth, friendliness, generosity and humour of the people. I maintain very strongly it is people, not places, which provide the key to successful travel. You can be staying in the most beautiful hotel in the world and still not have a memorable holiday.

In Nepal, a humble yak herder may invite you into his tiny home to meet his family. Or you may come across a village wedding or get to play a game of volleyball at a local school or sit around with a family at night and show them photos of your children over a shared glass of rice wine or cup of tea— simple and enriching pleasures that are sanctuaries from our over-complicated lives. Nepal has a great history of welcoming travellers, having traded with Tibet and other neighbours for thousands of years, and even today, visitors are always welcome.

However, my instant love affair with Nepal was to have ramifications I could never have imagined. In 1976, Goronwy and I decided to return to the Himalaya and to fund our trip we came up with the idea of leading a small tour. We stuck hand-made signs around the university campuses of Sydney and Canberra with almost instant results. The trip was a great success and the following year, people began ringing to see if we were planning another. We surveyed the travel industry and there wasn't really a product on the market we would buy and we believed that surely there were other travellers who felt as we did. So we registered a company in Canberra, Australian Himalayan Expeditions (AHE), cleared a bedroom in our house, purchased a typewriter and set up shop—with a starting capital of $250!

In those days, travelling to Everest was considered very unusual and highly adventurous and we were easily able to obtain coverage in the Canberra press of our early trekking forays.

The original, and enduring, philosophy of AHE was to give

people an intimate experience of the world's wild and beautiful places, travelling as the locals did, on foot. Later we extended this philosophy to include travel by camel, river raft, bicycle, elephant—anything that didn't involve motorised transport for the bulk of the trip. We even designed one holiday where clients trekked, cycled, rafted and travelled on camels, elephants and Arab dhows—all in the one itinerary! By cutting off our clients from everyday life as they knew it, our treks helped provide them with a different perspective. For a lot of people, these trips ended up having a significant impact on their lives.

What I find quite startling when I look back on the AHE story—which ended in 1988 when we sold the company—is that a country like Australia, with a small population and no mountains to speak of, was responsible for generating more trekkers to the Himalaya, at that time, than any other nation on earth. I believe AHE's success was fuelled by our passion for Nepal and our vision of what was possible there.

Although the way I travel has changed—as I have changed—Nepal continues to beguile me. Today, my relationship with the country is based on my work as the Royal Nepalese Honorary Consul-General. In this capacity, I am involved in raising funds for a number of community projects plus promoting tourism. It's nice to feel I can continue to make a contribution to a place which will always reside in my soul.

My son, Nima, who's named after Nima Tenzing Sherpa, a close friend of Goronwy's and mine, will be 18 this year and it's been a great joy to see him carry on the family's relationship with Nepal. He helped organise a school trip to the

Everest region last year and I feel sure he will always regard Nepal as having a special place in his heart.

It's a lot easier for people to access Nepal now than it was 20 years ago—in those pioneering days, there were no real environmental standards in place and operators such as ourselves faced a wide range of logistical challenges, such as not even being able to phone Nepal from Australia. Travellers today enjoy better service and have many more choices of treks. In recent years, areas that were previously closed to visitors—places such as Dolpo and Mustang—have opened their doors, offering a small number of trekkers an opportunity to witness people still living a traditional lifestyle.

I look forward to exploring these newly opened regions. I'm no longer interested in moving quickly through Nepal, or anywhere else for that matter. I think the secret to good travelling is to stop in a place and try to live as the locals do—if that means sitting with a book in a cafe in an historic city like Paris or Rome for a week, then so be it. At AHE, we used to say we were on a crusade to save people from the tyranny of the tinted coach window: such tours tend to isolate travellers from the countries they are visiting. I remember once going on a tour bus from Paris to the Palace of Versailles in France. I was so appalled by the sanitised commentary and constant microphone blaring, that I made it a one-way trip.

If it's enrichment you're after, be prepared to take the risk. Get off the bus and walk those bustling back streets. Be prepared to stop and let the place settle into your soul—slowly.

I have recently returned from my first trip to Italy. Even today, after so many tourists have plied its highways and byways, I still managed to find the Italian dream. I may not have seen all the sights but spent many hours shoulder-to-shoulder with the locals over morning coffee and tramped miles along cobbled streets steering clear of lines of bus tour passengers waiting, sometimes for hours, to go into museums. So, in a sense, I discovered Italy in the Nepalese way, by 'trekking', by keeping my time there as simple as possible and getting to know the locals.

Italy is a new passion but in the end, it's the warm smiles of Nepali people, the sight of tiny monasteries clinging to terraced hillsides and skeins of mountains which reside above the clouds that will always remain as my vision of paradise on earth. **"**

Ice
breaker

TIM BOWDEN
Broadcaster and author

"As a boy growing up in Tasmania, I was as close to Antarctica as it was possible to be in Australia. My father was a tremendous enthusiast of polar literature and at quite a young age, around twelve or thirteen, I read Nansen's *Farthest North,* a wonderful tale of exploration and high adventure in the Arctic. His ship, the *Fram,* was frozen in pack ice drifting back and forth for three years, while he overwintered with a companion in a stone hut hunting seals for food.

Stories like this engaged me tremendously and I was forever reminded of them as I watched the chartered Danish ships, sailing off down the Derwent towards Antarctica, with Australians on board

I even had my own Antarctic brush with fame. My grandfather, Frank Bowden, was the Director of Telegraphs in Hobart in 1912 when Amundsen beat Scott to the South Pole. Upon his return he sailed up the Derwent aboard the *Fram,* which he'd borrowed from Nansen, and had my grandfather take a telegram to the King of Norway to say that he had reached the Pole. So for some days my grandfather was the only person, other than the ship's company, to be aware of this incredible event. I still have a photograph of the *Fram* on the Derwent.

For all my enthusiasm, I never dreamt that I would ever visit Antarctica. It was one of the last great journeys on earth.

And it wasn't until the 1980s, when I was working with the Social History Unit of ABC Radio National, that I was able to further pursue my interest in the Antarctic. The then executive producer, Jenny Palmer, asked me to prepare six half-hour radio programs—*Australians in Antarctica*—an historical examination of the ANARE (Australian National Antarctic Research Expeditions) from 1947 onwards.

For it was just after the war that Australia first began mounting expeditions to Antarctica in order to justify our enormous claim—some 42 per cent—on the continent. The first attempt was made in 1948 in a little wooden tub called, improbably enough, *Wyatt Earp*, the last time an official expedition was to set off to Antarctica in a wooden ship with sails. The stories of her adventures were quite wonderful but she failed to make it to the continent.

An Australian expedition didn't actually reach mainland Antarctica until 1954 on a chartered Danish vessel, the ice-strengthened *Kista Dan*. Then began the whole wonderful adventure of exploration. Antarctica's coastline was mostly a dotted line on the map—nobody knew the main interior features. These visitors were genuine first-footers. They were aided and abetted in their explorations by husky dogs and crappy old World War II over-snow tractors.

I was utterly fascinated by these stories. Think of it: here we have a continent, effectively unknown more than halfway through the twentieth century. It was the last great adventure, and like all journalists I'm enormously attracted to good stories. This was a good story in every way: it had the lot. Except perhaps sex, but that came later. Women didn't get to the Antarctic continent until 1981. *Boys' Own* until then!

Most people are familiar with the so-called 'Heroic Era' of Antarctic exploration—Scott, Mawson, Shackleton and so on. But the post-war period was just as heroic. They had very limited equipment, very little money and the aircraft used in those early days were held together with little more than string and sealing wax in comparison to today.

Having completed the series of radio programs, I became very keen on visiting Antarctica myself. By the mid-'80s, the Antarctic Division was deploying larger ships with room for additional voyagers—artists, writers, journalists, film crews, politicians and so on. I approached the division with a package of offerings—the first *Backchat* of the year from Antarctica, pieces for Robyn Williams's *Science Show* and other articles—and I was on my way.

To quote a thundering tautology, you only have first-time experiences once. And I don't think anybody lucky enough to travel there by sea ever forgets their first voyage to Antarctica. Because, in a way, one is following in the footsteps of the original explorers, passing through storms of the Southern Ocean, which are quite incredible. These are the roughest seas in the world; enormous swells build as the westerly winds sweep around the continent. And while these seas are probably a lot less frightening nowadays, given the much stronger ships, there remains a tremendous sense of isolation. I think this is one of the reasons passengers cluster in the bar making merry and undergoing initiation ceremonies such as head shaving. It's one way of overcoming the feeling of being alone 'down there.'

For you *are* alone and that sense of isolation creeps up on you the further south you venture. Our bosun, Peter Hademak, who survived the loss of a ship in the Arctic, standing in a life raft, waist deep in freezing water for more than five hours, had no such thoughts of rescue in the Antarctic. 'If something went wrong down here, I'd simply jump overboard,' he said. 'Who's going to rescue me? There's no one here.' It's just you, and the sound of the sea and the wind. Howling wind. We had a Force 9 gale en route, the ship bucking and rearing, the spray crashing onto the bridge windows. It was very exciting.

It's tradition to take a lottery on board as to who will see the first iceberg and where on the horizon it will be. We've all seen photographs of icebergs but nothing prepares you for the real thing, this great soaring ice sculpture, decked with spires and turrets, that has broken away from the continent and is floating into the Southern Ocean to destruction. As the icebergs decay, they sometimes half roll over and great ice caves are visible around the base. If you are close enough, you can hear the sea booming in and out of these lovely blue translucent caverns.

After sailing through iceberg territory, the ship finally hits the pack ice, which from a distance looks nothing more than a white line on the horizon. The great bands of pack ice that encircle Antarctica have a dampening effect on the sea. The ship steadies immediately, and it is now that those prone to seasickness emerge, sometimes for the first time.

The ship is beset with strange sounds, a great clanging and banging as its ice-strengthened bow rides up and crashes through the floes, which are sometimes more than two metres thick. At the same time, wildlife begins to appear—seals and penguins, and the occasional whale. And at last the ship reaches the continent where a great curve of the ice sheet meets the sea and the Framnes Mountains, like the ribcage of a dinosaur, reach down the slope.

By this stage, the sun remains in the sky almost 24 hours a day, dipping below the horizon only briefly but long enough to turn on the most fabulous sunsets. Big Eye sets in. People having difficulty adjusting their sleep rhythms, wander about with large, bloodshot eyes. As opposed to Long Eye, which is

the look people get when they've been living in a small, isolated community for six months or longer. Long Eye has been
described as the 40-foot stare in the 10-foot room. Our on-
board doctor said he'd seen the same look in people who've
been through some sort of trauma.

Once arrived at Antarctica proper, I became instantly aware
that I was in one of the most tricky and dangerous places in the
world; that I was on the very edge of a very long supply line.
And I was very conscious of the fact that I had to be careful.
The first time I set foot on the continent is a case in point. I
jumped out of the helicopter and fell straight into a crevasse!
My leg smashed through the ice to my thigh. I stared down
into the blue depths and thought, 'This place is for real!'

From that moment, I placed my feet very carefully one in
front of the other. All the same, it's not always that easy.
Everything—other than the rock—is on the move in Antarctica; it's like a big dome of candied honey, the ice seeping
down to the edges of the continent, then breaking off and
floating away as icebergs.

Everyone is a visitor in Antarctica; even the professionals
are there for only one year. It's rather like venturing into
space; you have to take everything with you. And the sheer
enormousness of the place is quite overwhelming. Because
there's no pollution, you can see right to the horizon, there's
no sense of scale. If you spy a piece of rock sticking up
through the ice, it's hard to know if it's a mountain a hundred
kilometres away or just a piece of rock. There is nothing available to make a size comparison—no trees, no houses. This
can be very disconcerting for pilots. With nothing but blue
skies and white ice, it's impossible to know, without checking

the instruments, whether you are ten or two thousand metres above the ice cap. They describe it as a 'vague out'.

Phillip Law, who was the first director of the Australian Antarctic Division, from 1949 to 1966, says no one comes back from Antarctica, even from a short visit, unchanged. He explains that living at such close quarters makes you more tolerant of other people's idiosyncrasies, and the sheer immensity and overpowering effect of the environment forces a confrontation of the bigger issues—immortality, your place in nature, the nature of this world and of the universe. I would not jib at using the words 'spiritual experience'. I am not a religious person, but there is no doubt that in a philosophical and reflective way, Antarctica causes you to think about why we are here, and the fragility of the planet.

Nothing decays in Antarctica. On one of our little expeditions we flew out from Mawson in a helicopter and found some rations, among other junk, that had been left there by a party stranded by crevasses in 1967. We opened the packages and found a MacRobertsons chocolate bar looking as it did on the day it was manufactured with its pictures of the Tower of London and the pyramids. There were some rolled oats that were still crumbly. Back at the station we ate melon-and-ginger jam left over from the supplies in 1954.

The cosmic splendour of Antarctica and its wildlife is one thing; what makes its human residents tick is another. How do they cope, or not cope, as may be the case? Antarctica inspires a tremendous recidivism; people return again and again. One expeditioner, Graeme 'Chompers' Currie, has spent eleven winters on the continent and made countless summer visits.

There's something that keeps drawing people back—it's partly social: the idea of getting together with a group of people and living a life which is removed from everyday society. People can make their own rules—up to a point. But when the darkness of winter comes down, as the division's head of polar medicine, Des Lugg, once said to me, 'The Australian stations remain as isolated as were the classic expeditions of Scott, Shackleton and Mawson, and the Antarctic remains an extremely dangerous place to live and work.'

If anything happens they must cope alone. No one can come to their aid. There's a cycle, apparently, of elation and depression. When the first ship arrives everyone is full of joy to be there. When the ship departs there's an immediate dip in the graph. Mid-winter is a time of traditional celebration, with formal dinners and bawdy pantomimes. Then there's another dip as everyone realises they are, after all, only halfway through their tenure. The return of the wildlife brings an enormous psychological boost, and by the time the ship returns to take the expeditioners home, everyone is riding high once again.

Some, however, don't welcome the ship's return and find it a huge wrench to be plunged back into everyday life. People venture to Antarctica for many reasons. Some like the service-style life, and ordered existence, a positive prison, a self-imposed exile. Adventure, I'm happy to say, still plays an important role. Others venture south to escape unhappy relationships. Scientists, of course, have specialist reasons for visiting.

An Antarctic station community is divided between 'boffins'—the scientists—and 'tradies' who keep the place running: diesel mechanics, plumbers, carpenters and cooks. Sometimes a kind of us-and-them situation arises, but not always. You can have your sensitive new age tradesperson as well as your ocker boffin!

My life is now quite intrinsically linked to Antarctica. For the last three years I've been working on the history of ANARE, which is 50 years old this year. It's called *The Silence Calling*, an evocative phrase I took from a recently discovered poem written by Sir Douglas Mawson. That is also the title of a documentary I have written and narrated for the ABC, looking at what Australians have been doing in Antarctica during the last half century.

Most of the good Antarctic titles have been used—lots of references to ice. Mawson's own *Home of the Blizzard* was a superb title. 'And if perchance you hear the silence calling', wrote Sir Douglas in his poem. That really appealed to me. However, his last line, referring to 'the brotherhood of men that know the south', is less ideologically appropriate now that women expeditioners regularly go there. Something in Antarctica does keep calling people back, and it could well be the silence, for silence actually exists in Antarctica.

An ABC sound recordist colleague once succeeded in recording total silence out on the ice cap. I can't vouch for the value of this exercise in radio terms, but I do know it's possible. The silence certainly still calls me. I've become a recidivist: an Antarctic recidivist. **"**

The power
of nature

JANE HOLMES
Journalist

"We went to Africa to shoot stories for *Talk to the Animals* and I think it was simply the power of nature that made me fall instantly in love with the continent. During endless drives between locations, the glimpses of animals I had only seen in zoos or read about in childhood books just took my breath away.

I expected to be a little blasé about seeing African animals in the wild for the first time, but when I saw them running free it almost reduced me to tears because this is where they belong. For someone who has a passionate love of animals, it was a very moving experience.

My very first African safari was in South Africa's Pilansberg National Park, adjoining the glitz and glamour and casinos of the infamous Sun City. We were picked up at around 5.30 am and driven through the dusty bush, past acacia trees, a typical African landscape. I remember Andy Laidlaw, the sound recordist, was the first person to see an animal, a giraffe. I distinctly recall thinking, 'Where?' and I then realised that not only were these animals extremely large but they were also masters of camouflage.

One of my most moving experiences happened on that first safari. We saw a white rhino and her calf as they bolted across the track in front of our jeep. All of a sudden, there they were, these amazing prehistoric creatures straight out of *Jurassic Park*. Then they disappeared into the bushes. It was quite magnificent.

Next we flew to Zimbabwe, where we stayed at Malalangwe Lodge, in the Matopos Hills, a few hours' drive from Bulawayo. It is run by Richard Peeke, a former game warden of the Matopos National Park, and his wife, Bookey, and it has these perfect little stone cabins with thatched roofs studded up the side of a rocky outcrop behind the main lodge and the pool. The cabins blend perfectly into the landscape and you feel very much at home with the environment, even though you are staying in guest facilities.

Richard and Bookey make you feel as if you are guests in their own home, and it was through their astounding knowledge, compounded by their love for the animals and for their environment, that I got to learn more about the real Africa. They had bought land devastated by farming, restored the natural ecosystem, and repopulated it with the animals that were there thousands of years before man took over.

This was also where I experienced my first African sunrise. Researcher Mary Rose Trainor and I were sharing a cabin at the very top of the outcrop, and as we woke, the sun's rays gently kissing the ancient hills around us, we heard this strange scrabbling sound outside. We opened the door for a better view, only to be confronted by David Rose, the cameraman, there to shoot the sunrise. He nearly died of fright when he saw reporter and researcher, with that early morning look about them, mascara-stained cheeks and nighties slightly askew. A beautiful experience with nature and a scary one for the cameraman!

The Matopos Hills are made up of amazing rock formations, weathered by thousands of years of wind and rain, big dome-shaped rocks, like huge marbles, jutting up forever. As we walked around this strange land, we discovered the ultimate tourist attraction: the Lizard Man. This sprightly and ancient character has lived there all his life and wears what appears to be a scout's uniform, encrusted with badges from every country in the universe.

He led us to Cecil Rhodes's grave, at the top of a particularly large, steep, rocky outcrop, squatted down and took out these maize balls which he rolled between his fingers as he called out in Shona, the local dialect. Before we could blink, a swarm of small rainbow-coloured lizards teemed out of the surrounding rocks and crevices, gathering at his feet as he talked to them.

He put a maize ball down and the lizards rushed over and started throwing the ball around. Before we knew it, he'd got a soccer match going, complete with commentary: Zimbabwe versus Botswana! An unsuspecting elephant shrew, which looks a bit like a mouse complete with a little trunk, blundered into the midst of the mêlée and became part of his commentary as he shouted, 'C'mon the mouse!' It was quite a spectacle.

Leaving Richard and Bookey was like saying goodbye to family, but we had places to go. We spent some time in Harare, where we visited the Lion and Cheetah Park and met an amazing man called Viv Bristow, who has lived with animals all his life, working with big cats for movies, including *The Gods Must Be Crazy*. We had chatted to Viv and his wife, Carole, for an hour when he finally said, 'Have a look behind the sofa', and there were two little lion cubs. They'd been there all the time and were looking up at us, rather sternly, with amazing baby blue eyes. When we patted them, we soon discovered that these little balls of fluff, with their sweet eyes and tiny miaows, were really tiny fur-coated balls of steel. They were *so* strong, and it made me realise how a lion could rip an animal apart with one swipe of its paw.

After a long, dusty drive to Lake Kariba, we arrived just as our launch pulled out. We yelled, they turned, we raced aboard and settled down, with a sigh of relief, for the ride to Fothergill Island. We were treated to the most magical sunset: vivid reds and oranges that seemed to linger forever. It was a balmy evening, and the further the launch went out onto the lake the more strident the colours became. All you could see on the horizon were the silhouettes of dead trees and the twinkling lights of the fishing boats. It may sound overly dramatic, but right there and then I really did feel completely at one with nature and the universe.

We stayed in beautifully appointed cabins on Fothergill, and the wildlife and birdlife were prolific. There were more beautiful sunsets, including one at the end of a very long day's shooting. We were on our way back to camp, approaching a rise, when David stopped the vehicle and got the camera set up just as a herd of impala trotted gracefully up the hill, stopped right in the centre of the massive glowing red and gold orb of the setting sun, turned to look at us for a fleeting moment, and bounded over the hill. Hollywood couldn't have staged a more stunning scene.

We flew out of Fothergill in a charter aircraft from the landing strip easily recognisable as the soccer ground in the movie *The Power of One*, and headed for a very brief stop at Victoria Falls. This is where the Zambezi River goes over a chasm about 1.7 kms wide and drops about 110 metres. You understand the unadulterated power of nature when you see mega millions of litres of water gushing over this chasm. The roar can be heard from kilometres away. You can also see the mist that rises above the Falls, known in the local vernacular as 'Mosi Wa Tunya', which means 'the smoke that thunders'.

We shot the Falls from a helicopter flown by a wonderful top gun pilot. With a film permit, you are allowed to fly very low, and we got so close that David came back with leaves in his sneakers. We even sent a few whitewater rafters ducking for cover as we flew up the river. Seeing the magnitude of the Falls and the river was exhilarating—you could understand how David Livingstone, the Scottish missionary and explorer, felt when he discovered it and said, 'It is sights like these that must have been gazed upon by angels in their flight.' It is one of those experiences that etches itself into your soul. We had such a brief time at Victoria Falls that later that day it seemed like the most powerful and vivid dream I've ever had.

From there we drove into Botswana and boarded a charter aircraft which took us into the heart of the Okavango Delta. The Okavango is the world's largest inland delta, covering some 15,000 square kilometres, and can be seen from space. The area is well managed in that the number and size of camps is very limited. We touched down on a very small and dusty landing strip and were met by an equally dusty driver and jeep, who took us through the bush to the private camp of *National Geographic* documentary maker Tim Liversedge and his photographer wife, June.

Tim is one of the world's best documentary makers, and he and June spend months, even years, just looking at one group or species of animals. He made a wonderful documentary on a very rare and endangered bird called the Pel's fishing owl, the world's largest owl, and in the course of the documentary he found an abandoned chick which he raised. His name is Henley, and, although free to leave, he chooses to live with Tim at the camp. He is the most beautiful owl you could ever see, perfectly spherical, a chubby chap, with great big wide black eyes, and he peers down at you with a very judgmental look. At various times Henley would cry out 'ohhhh noooo', almost as if he didn't quite approve of what he was seeing.

We spent a couple of days with Henley, but on the last day I think I may have scarred him emotionally for life. I'd just removed my clothing and was about to jump into the shower when I realised I was not alone. I looked up and my eyes met Henley's. He looked at me, horrified, screeched 'ohhhh noooo' and left rather hurriedly. I felt totally rejected and he's now in therapy, I believe.

Tim and June have a couple of tents for visitors. David, Andy and our other reporter, Steve Oemcke, got the regular tents but Mary Rose and I were treated to what Tim laughingly termed the 'Honeymoon Suite'. It was a huge tent erected on a wooden platform on stilts, with a balcony at one end overlooking the Delta. There were two perfectly carved and embossed seats, the ultimate deckchairs, from which you could gaze at a beautiful vista of palm trees and papyrus reeds, water channels weaving through. It was like looking at infinity. There were the most beautiful noises throughout the day, a whole symphony of bird calls, particularly in the early morning, and at night there were various rumblings and a variety of mysterious and unidentified noises. You are never alone, and it's never, ever silent, despite the fact that you are in the middle of nowhere.

At the end of one day's shooting, Tim took us out in a boat. We turned off the motor as the sun set and sat, looking at perfect mirror images of little palm-tree-studded islets in the gently rippling waters, when suddenly we heard something crashing around and the snapping of branches and trees. It turned out to be a wild elephant, which broke through the papyrus, stopped right in front of us, raised its trunk, trumpeted a perfect scale and then just carried on through the rushes. That was our first close encounter with a wild elephant—absolutely spine-tingling.

But that was just a warm-up, because our next destination was Abu's Camp, which offers elephant-back safaris. The camp is run by Randall Jay Moore, who looks a little like Groucho Marx—he always has a cigar in his mouth and his wild hair is tied back in a ponytail. He's an American, an ex-circus trainer who did a bit of an about-face when he rescued elephants from America and other parts of the globe and relocated them to Botswana. They weren't set free because, having been captive for so many years, these animals have no survival skills, but Randall Jay Moore has given them a new home in more natural surroundings.

There is a team of elephants from a range of backgrounds but the camp is named after the star of the show, Abu, well known as the elephant who features in Peekay's dream in the movie version of *The Power of One* and in *White Hunter, Black Heart* with Clint Eastwood.

In between movies, Abu and the other adults take clients on safaris. You sit on the back of an elephant, in a howdah with a mahout at the helm, while experiencing what it is like to be part of a herd. The idea is to see Africa in the most genuine way possible, allowing a natural interaction with other wild animals. The herd includes a gaggle of young orphans who've bonded to the adult elephants—they're affectionately known as the Brat Pack.

The adults travel in line while the babies tag alongside, acting like a little pack of hoons, running off into the bushes, playing with each other or mock charging some unsuspecting warthog, before trotting back to the elephant with which they've bonded. It's just like watching a pack of very naughty schoolchildren.

On our last morning, we made our way to a waterhole where we were going to swim with the elephants, a prospect which was both terrifying and exhilarating, but an experience I was not about to knock back. I had to sit bareback, which is no mean feat because it's very hard keeping your legs that far apart for any length of time! I was determined not to fall off, so I sat on the elephant, sandwiched, a mahout behind me, hanging on for grim death to Michael, our guide in front. Unfortunately, because of the motion of the elephant, the resulting footage of me on the elephant in between these two muscular men looked rather pornographic!

While the accommodation is in five-star tents, dining at Abu's Camp is silver service and *al fresco*, with the table laid with linen and silverware on the banks of a waterhole, stars glimmering in the sky, campfire burning as you listen to the night noises. Being so far from city lights, you can see satellites clearly in the night sky. Shooting stars, too, are a regular sight.

First thing in the morning, we heard what appeared to be a baritone having a fit, sort of a 'wahoo, wahoo', which turned out to be baboons. The other regular sound was like a very stiff breeze going through trees, but it turned out to be a wild elephant roaming in for a feed. Which is fine, except it was shaking the trees immediately above our tent—again making me realise I was leading a pretty precarious existence.

The last port of call was a real contrast to Abu's Camp. From five-star luxury we had to take a teensy weensy, terrifying aircraft across the Delta to Gunn's Camp, run by Mike Gunn and his Australian-born wife, Lindy. Gunn's Camp was very comfortable and, in a strange way, because it's not luxurious, you feel more in tune with what's around you. Whereas at Abu's Camp we travelled around on elephants, at Gunn's Camp we went by boat—either a large dinghy with an outboard or by canoe, called a makoro, which is the Okavango Delta's version of the gondola.

The main memory I have of this part of the Okavango is seeing my first firefly. When the sun set, the ground suddenly appeared to have developed atomic pimples, which turned out to be fireflies—tiny balls of phosphorescence which, when they settled on the ground, you could catch. It was just like holding a shining star in my hand.

I live in a tiny little house in a cramped and polluted suburb, in a sophisticated and civilised part of the world. And in Africa I'd left that behind and found somewhere as poles apart as I could ever get: vast areas of dust and huge herds of wild animals. To be walking in their territory and breathing the same air, that was the charm and the pull of the place. And not knowing what was going to happen next, but realising, whatever it was, we were in for a very great adventure.

I fell in love with the spirit of adventure and the promise of what the day held for us, and I was never disappointed. I'd go back again in a moment, just to try and recapture that feeling. And I know I would, the moment the plane landed. **"**

The moment I stepped off the plane

MIKE WHITNEY
TV presenter

"I went off to India for the first time in 1984, and from the moment I stepped off the plane I thought it was extraordinary. I'd taken six months off because of a knee injury and, before I left Australia, I arranged to meet up with two really good mates of mine, Greg Charlwood and his wife, Karen, and another mate, Tony White, who was taking his wife, Mary, on honeymoon to India. I travelled through South Africa and Europe before flying to Bombay; the others had been travelling through Asia. I gave them my flight details but when I flew into Bombay I thought the chances of finding them were minimal. It was about one in the morning and I'll always remember seeing this multitude of people—hawkers selling things, beggars, bodies sleeping everywhere.

I thought it was ugly, nasty, but *everything* was just *happening*. I was beginning to get worried when, out of nowhere, this head appeared above the crowd, arms waving madly, and it was my buddy, Greg. I was so glad to see him because I was stunned. In an instant, I'd realised what was meant by culture shock.

Next day we looked around Bombay, which really blew me away, but we caught a train to Delhi the following day because the monsoon was coming. It started raining the night before we left, and by the time we got up in the morning half the place was flooded, the gutters were overflowing and the trenches along the side of the street were running with putrid water.

I recall the train trip well because I shared a carriage with four Indians, one a Sikh. I knew this was a different religion but I didn't really understand it. There were three beds on one side and two on the other, and I remember this Sikh guy getting changed to get into bed. He undid his turban and then his hair and it just fell down around his shoulders, then he undid his beard. I was mesmerised, and I asked him about being a Sikh, and the other guys, all university students, joined in the conversation. They asked if I was travelling alone and I told them about my friends. One asked if they had children so I told him, no, they'd been travelling around Asia and, anyway, she was on the Pill. I had to explain contraceptives to them and they freaked out, saying it was not God's will, and this was not the way it should be. My thoughts at that stage were, 'Hang on, if you knew a bit more about this subject, there wouldn't be a billion people running around in India and everybody would have a feed.' But they made me understand it was not in their consciousness to think that way, it would be going against God's will, which is to sleep together and have children, and that is the way it is meant to be. But it's created so many problems for them.

I'd been in New Delhi for a few days and one morning I was walking around Connaught Place, this big plaza area, and there were two children lying dead in the gutter. One was about three, the other a baby about six months old, and people were just stepping over them and not batting an eyelid. For me—I was 25—it was a really shocking experience.

I've heard it said that when you go to India, it cleanses your soul. To me, that sums up exactly how people from the Western world should view it. You have to accept what's happening and why, and develop an understanding of Indian religion and culture. I followed a beggar one day, taking lots of photos of him. He begged all day and we'd been moving in and out of Connaught Place and finally he walked into a Hindu temple. He'd made about 25 rupees over the day, that's less than two dollars, and he walked in, gave half to the temple and walked out, taking the remaining money home with him. He was so strong in his belief in what he was doing and how the Hindu gods will protect and look after him.

I walked out and thought about Western greed. We don't get ice in our drinks and we're spewing, we sit down in a restaurant and the service is slow and we complain. If we don't earn a grand a week, we haven't got a good job. Most people in India, like that beggar, have got almost *nothing*, and they're happy to give it away. Being in India does cleanse your soul and now I really appreciate what I have in Australia.

That first visit, we travelled around and saw Bombay, Delhi, Jaipur and Agra. The Taj Mahal was fascinating and I think anybody who's disappointed by it must be very hard to please. Looking down those long gardens that lead up to it, the white Taj shimmering in the sun, the river behind it—I remember thinking, 'How perfect!' Then when I got up close and actually saw the inlaid marble, carved with such precision . . . what unbelievable craftsmanship.

My favourite place in India is Kashmir. We stayed on Dal Lake in Srinagar on this old, wooden, English-style house-boat, the size of a house with three bedrooms, beautiful furniture, fully carpeted, the old silver service, and it cost around $5 a day for the five of us including food. Every day there was a knock at the door, you'd open it and walk out and there'd be the lake and there'd be a man with a little canoe full of all kinds of fruits and vegetables. Half an hour later, another knock on the door and it'd be the tailor who's got his sewing machine in the boat, plus shirts, trousers, materials, and says he'll be back in two hours with more samples. Whatever you wanted to buy was peddled, continuously throughout the day, from hundreds of little shikara boats crisscrossing the lake.

On the last day of Ramadan, we went into Srinagar and the locals were saying it was going to be a big night. They'd told us about a street where nothing but firecrackers were sold and there were these rickety old wooden buildings, chock-a-block full of firecrackers, and I'm talking thunderers—these things were half a stick of dynamite, rockets a metre tall. So we spent the equivalent of about $15 and went back to the houseboat with a large bag full of firecrackers.

That night, when the sun went down, we got onto the roof of the houseboat and started letting them off. The rockets were like the things you see on New Year's Eve. They'd go off with a huge whoosh and then . . . poof . . . into a big five-metre star deal. Some of the wicks were dodgy and would just fizz, and we'd be thinking, 'If this thing goes off, it'll blow the boat to smithereens.' If the wick died out, the boat boy would appear, saying, 'Give me the matches, I will light'. He thought it was great! Then all these boats appeared out of nowhere and everyone was yelling, 'Last night of Ramadan! Fireworks!' There were about 50 boats around us and every time we let something off, the crowd would go, 'Ahhhhh!' So I got one of the really big thunder things, lit it and just shot it off the edge into the boats. It was pretty irresponsible but very funny, and people were just diving into the water. We stayed on for a week and everyone on the lake was still talking about it.

From Kashmir, we trekked up to Gulmarg and Alpather. One day we trekked from our camp up to this huge plateau where the mountain just rises in front of you. The camp was about 9,000 feet above sea level, and when you get over 10,000 feet you aren't supposed to do more than one or two thousand feet a day because of altitude sickness. But we kept walking, and climbed to 17,000 feet by lunchtime. We started to struggle. Our guide must have been 75 years old, and the higher we got the more frequent our breaks because we were gasping for air. We'd stop for a drink and this old guy would crash out on the grass. When we were ready, he'd get straight up and start walking—he could fall asleep at the drop of a hat. He told us he did that walk twice a week and it was a good 10-hour trek, hard work, virtually straight up, following donkey trails and over the other side to the frozen lake. It was the demarcation line between Kashmir and Pakistan, and we were warned not to go down because they were flinging a few salvos across the border at each other. You could hear in the distance, way down in the valley, the occasional 'whump' of rockets or gunfire. So we backpedalled and returned the way we had come.

Another time, we trekked up to Kolahoi Glacier and walked along the top—a spectacular vista. I'd never been that close to high mountain peaks before, and these were 20,000 feet, covered in snow and really rugged. It was cold and we camped out in tents and slept on the edge of rivers. That trek goes down as one of the most amazing experiences of my life.

We found this little hut and a man lived way up there on his own and sold drinks, chocolate bars and nibblies. We asked if there was anything to eat and he told us he had some chickens. There were around 30 free-range chickens pecking their way around the place. I said, 'That would be good mate, barbecue one for us.' I'll never forget him, sneaking out, knife behind his back like a cartoon character, and these chickens *knew*, they just took off. He finally got one and whang, off with its melon. He plucked it, cooked it, and we ate it that night. It was by far the best-tasting chook I've ever had in my life.

When I returned to India, it was to play cricket. It's always different when you're with a team because you are under constraints, every day is mapped out for you and they don't really like you wandering off. I was glad I'd seen India before, and every time I think about it I remember that first time, when I saw it from the underside. That's really what the country is about—there's more downside than upside, and it's how the country fits together that's so fascinating.

I played at Braebourne Stadium, in Bombay, home to the Cricketers' Club of India now. I've been in cricket clubs all around the world and this is *the* most elaborate pavilion I've ever seen, with inlaid marble and tapestry on the walls, Louis XV chairs, and it's something like US$100,000 to join the club and US$30,000 a year, and there's a thirty-year waiting list. The difference between the 95 per cent who live on the street and earn a few dollars and these suckers who make up five per cent of the population and have 90 per cent of the wealth, is just extraordinary.

I loved playing cricket against the Indians—they are that fanatical about the game, it's beyond belief. I never went on a full tour with the Australian team but they knew who I was. People would recognise me at home but I was never a super-star. In India, however, they would stop me and say, 'Mike Whitney, 427 wickets . . .' and recite all the statistics, my best performances, all my personal details. 'You are coming from Sydney, you are being born in Crown Street Women's

Hospital . . .' Because they read players' profiles in cricket magazines, and can just quote all this stuff. If there's a game on, the ground's always packed out, people waiting to get in. And the bribery and corruption! Nine times out of ten, the guy who prints the tickets does two sets and there are ten thousand people outside, clamouring to get in. There are video shops in India, as big as some of the large ones in Sydney, and all they rent is *cricket* videos.

The game's a really big part of their life. Kapil Dev and players like him, they're treated like gods, they'll never have to work, never want for anything. The Indians don't seem to subscribe to the tall poppy syndrome—if you're a legend and you've achieved that through cricket or whatever, you really are a legend. Not like here, where it's a case of 'lucky bastard'. Some Indian cricketers are among the greatest in the world, so I think they deserve to be revered.

I really like Indian people, and one thing I've learned about them is that they don't like to embarrass you. The sideways nod is endemic and it covers a multitude of responses. I toured with a bloke called Bruce Yardley and he relates a funny story about getting into a Bombay cab and telling the driver, 'I've broken my watch strap and I want to go to Colaba Markets', and the driver says, 'Oh, no, sahib, not very good.' So Bruce says, 'Listen, the concierge told me that's the best place to go.' 'Oh no, no, no,' says the driver, so Bruce insists, 'Hey, do you want the fare or don't you?' 'No problem, sahib.' They get to the market and there's nothing happening, so the driver turns around and says, 'See? Closed!' So Bruce says, 'Why didn't you tell me?' and the driver answers, 'I am *trying* to tell you but you are telling me to go to Colaba

Markets and I am telling you no good.' Things like that happen all the time.

People ask me why I like it so much. There are so many places I like—Lizard Island, New Zealand, Bermuda. I really love the West Indies. But India to me is just so different, it's like being on another planet. There is always a possibility things can go drastically wrong and I like a bit of an adrenalin flow. It's so different to our lifestyle, our mentality, it's right at the other end of the scale.

Every day when I was in India, I would walk onto the street wondering what I was going to see—a camel trotting past, elephants loaded up with gear, some dude with a mongoose and a cobra, some unbelievable piece of architecture, people sleeping or cooking by the side of the road. Every day I knew I was going to see something that would blow my mind. India had always enchanted me, but the reality far exceeded my wildest dreams. To people who've never been there, it's very hard to explain. **"**

Chapter 4

ANCESTRAL TIES

Today's Australians and
their mother countries

The Italian connection

VINCE SORRENTI
Comedian

"My father came to Australia in 1952, when he was nineteen, and lived with another Italian guy who introduced him to his sister, when she came out in 1954, and Dad married her. They're both from Calabria in Southern Italy. Mum's from a town called Rocella Ionica, on the Ionic Coast, and Dad's from the Tyrrhenian side of Calabria, from a village called Cirello, which is very rural.

The two towns are only a few kilometres apart, not a great distance, but there are some minor cultural differences. Both are in Reggio di Calabria and within that province, a few words will change from town to town and the accents vary, but they are pretty much the same. 'Italy' is really just an administrative word—the country's actually composed of twenty very different regions. The Romans, for example, are nothing like the Venetians. People living in towns fifty kilometres apart will use different words to each other.

In the late 1940s and early 1950s in Italy, people weren't starving, but they recognised there was very little opportunity to get ahead. They existed under a feudal system with a baron who owned the land which people worked and, in exchange, they got to use some of his land for themselves. They milked goats, made their own cheese, grew tomatoes and olives. My dad still does this, using the land as something he has to get a yield out of—and he lives in Concord, in the suburbs of Sydney. If the capitalist system ever collapsed, you could still get a good feed at his house. He grows everything in his backyard—lettuces, tomatoes, broccoli, eggplants, garlic, grapes for wine, olives: unbelievable what you can get out of a suburban block.

Mum and Dad both came to Australia on the same basis—

as free settlers—and they each had to scrounge all the money they could possibly get their hands on to pay their way out here. Italian migration operated under a certain system: the father and the eldest son would always leave first, a year or two ahead. They would work and set up a base in Australia and then the rest of the family would follow. Dad was the eldest son so he came out first and it was pretty much the same on Mum's side. The reason migrant suburbs developed was because these people hung together. Travelling to Australia must have been like going to Mars: on a boat for forty days and getting off on the other side of the world. Some of these people had never travelled more than a donkey's ride from home. My mum hadn't known anything beyond the next village, which was five kilometres from where she lived.

They weren't necessarily excited by the prospect of Australia. They saw leaving Italy as something they had to do if they were ever going to get ahead or prosper. A lot of stories would float back from Italians already settled in Australia: they would brag about how unreal it was. They would make out the streets were paved with gold, that it was the land of milk and honey. My uncle, who Dad lived with at first, was such a clown. He'd say, 'I don't even wash the dishes, I just throw them out the window!' Really he was just so lazy that he would eat off paper plates! There were lots of stories like that. But, really, they all worked their butts off when they got here. They had to work in factories and on the railways, as builders' labourers, in road gangs—pretty hard yakka. Dad did all that, so did Mum in later years. They didn't come here and have it easy.

Most migrants who came to Australia at that time hung on to values that were really old. The majority left Italy or

Greece in the late 1940s or early 1950s and pretty much continued to abide by the customs and social norms of that time. That's why you see so many problems with my generation. Kids from those Italian families have grown up wanting to be more liberated, expecting different lives for women, demanding more opportunities, but this is also true of young people living in Italy. My parents find this odd: they expect things in Italy to have remained the way they were when they left. But they, like many migrants of their generation, have hung on to the old values, even though things have changed so much in Italy.

I was brought up in Punchbowl [in suburban Sydney] and I was fourteen the first time I went to Italy. My parents' generation remember only the hardships and most of them wouldn't go back to the old country for all the tea in China, but I go to Italy every year. It's got the fifth biggest economy in the world, but the Italians here [of my parents' vintage] think it's just like it was at the end of the war. I remember in the '60s and early '70s, Mum would send survival packs to her relatives filled with coffee—Italian coffee!—and socks, and tea towels of the Opera House. Can you imagine them opening the parcels and finding coffee and socks?

So, the first time, I didn't really want to go. I thought it would be like entering the Middle Ages. I imagined there'd be people pulling drays. When I got there, my cousin was riding around on a Moto Guzzi. I thought it was all fantastic and wondered how I could have been so hoodwinked. My folks didn't see it that way, even though they saw how well everyone was doing.

Life in Italy is more qualitative than in Australia. You can make more money here, but they enjoy a better quality of life. They eat better, they dress better, they live in more beautiful houses, even though they may not have the space we do. We may drive a bigger car, and have a bigger bank account, but when you measure a country's standard of living, it shouldn't just be based on economic prosperity.

I found Italy really tugged on my heart strings, particularly when I visited where Mum and Dad had grown up. I went to Dad's village and it was a real backwater with dirt streets. He pointed out the house where he'd grown up and it was a hovel, the whole thing no bigger than an Australian lounge room. Eight kids lived there but the lifestyle was healthier than ours: hardly any meat, goat's milk, wholegrain bread, fresh fish and fruit. The migrants encountered health problems in Australia, eating meat three times a day and drinking grog. Excess comes with its pitfalls.

Mum's village, Rocella Ionica, is a semi-historical place in Calabria. It's a medieval fortress on a hill and the whole town used to be inside that fortress. Mum's grandparents had stories that if you weren't inside by dusk, the doors would close and that was it. These tales were passed down through the generations and that's largely what it would have been like in medieval times. The whole known world was a pretty lawless place. Everyone had to be in the domain of a lord or baron who had knights to defend you. If the walls weren't big enough, someone could come and take your town.

This particular fortress is pretty dilapidated now, over-run by sheep and goats and wild grasses, but as I was standing on it, looking out over the town, I felt that but for the grace of God I could have grown up right there. It was a really weird feeling. One of the dilemmas my generation has is this sense of not really belonging. I was born in Australia but I'm very Italian and yet when I go to Italy, I feel very Australian.

Even with the progress in multiculturalism in this country, people still don't see me as an Australian. I'm so Australian it's a joke! Yet in some people's eyes I will never be an Aussie. But I can honestly say that being who I am has never prevented me from doing what I want to do. My Mum goes down to the local club and pulls the pokies and drinks Bundy and Coke; she speaks with a heavy Italian accent but she's pretty Aussie, really. For her generation, the thought of going back is out of the question.

But members of my generation have rediscovered the old country and we see it in a different way. I love Italy—I visit there every year. I've recently become an Italian citizen—that means I am a European citizen, a part of fifteen countries— but I'm also an Australian.

Among European countries, Italy has been extraordinarily successful. There was an economic revolution in the '60s and a semi-industrial rural backwater has become a powerhouse. Most Italian-Australians don't realise this. They've never seen other parts of Europe; they grew up in small towns and Italy, to most, was Calabria or even their own neighbourhood. Whereas I've been everywhere in Italy—to many places several times—and I intend to buy a house and live on the Italian Riviera. I've got a contract to write a book there and while I'll never completely leave Australia, it's nice to be somewhere else, to see this country objectively. That distance will allow me to write very cleanly about Australia.

Portofino is my favourite place in the world. I have tried to go back there every year since I was fourteen. It's on the Riviera di Levante, just south of Genoa in the region of Liguria.

It has real topographical drama: steep hills, beautiful bays. It's like a millionaires' playground. I want to get a house in the next little bay along from Portofino in a town called Camogli, which is short for Casi dei Mogli, which means 'homes of the wives'. It's the next best-known town on the Riviera after Portofino and its neighbour, Santa Margherita, and lies north of that famous pair, just around a point.

Portofino is a marvellous example of the way Italians design housing. In Sydney we are most concerned with the view, with how much we can see, we never consider the people looking at us. It's all huge, tall obstructions on the landscape here whereas in Italy, it's exactly the reverse. Italians will build along the form of the landscape, so whether you've got a view or not is irrelevant. It's how your house looks from the water, the way it blends into the topography that's important.

Camogli is equally as beautiful as Portofino. It's just gorgeous, all narrow streets and arches, painted in oranges and yellows and browns. And there are lots of lovely little beaches. The Genovese are renowned for being tight-arsed. Where we would say 'Let's go Dutch', the Italians say, 'Let's go Genovese'. There is a famous joke—there are two Genovese in a restaurant and they're arguing over who is going to pay, so the waiter comes out and puts a big bowl of water on the table and says, 'Both of you put your heads in the water; the first one who comes up has to pay the bill.' And, of course, they both drown. To break this notion, twice a year in Camogli they have a joke that everyone who goes there eats for free. They put this gigantic frying pan in the town square—it's huge, and they have a giant fish fry and feed everyone.

All the little towns in Italy have at least one tradition such as that. The history, culture, the richness in food, ideas, it's simply beautiful. I've really learned to love Liguria. It's where pesto comes from, and fettuccine, too. It's also the home of foccacia, and is famous for nuts—pine nuts, hazelnuts—and lots of liqueurs, also spaghetti sauces made with liqueurs, and sauces with walnuts and cream. It's very different from Calabria which is famous for mainly vegetarian produce like capers, capsicum, chickpeas and all those fiery red sauces, but they do eat goat in Calabria and there is fantastic seafood. As you move further north, you get rice and butter replacing oil and pasta and then polenta instead of pasta.

'Italian' as we know it was popularised by Dante. He wrote in Siennese and this became known as Italian. Now, even Siennese is a different language than it was in Dante's time. It's wonderful how things change and evolve, and the richness that develops. Now there is an official Italian language. In my parents' generation, when there wasn't TV, they only spoke Calabresi—it's a bit of an effort for my Mum to speak Italian, even now. Dad spoke Italian as well as Calabresi, but my Mum struggled with Italian and English. These days you can go from rural Sicily to the high industrial and financial areas of Milan and there will be not much difference. There will be changes in tonality and accent, but they're basically speaking the same language.

But the old people speak the original language which should never be lost to us. There are books and songs in Calabresi which just make me cry. It's so overwhelmingly beautiful but there are only a few people left in the world who know what is being said and why.

Part of my architectural degree was to spend a year away

from university and either work or travel, but to pass that year I had to write a report. I went to Italy and wrote about urban design and the way a city lives with its space, the way society needs architecture. There were some beautiful examples of piazzas in Italy which I bisected for days. People would just wander, guys walking arm-in-arm, then lovers would meet, and if you didn't walk the square at night, you simply didn't exist. I drew a map of the square showing all its functions and activities. On a larger scale, that interaction relates to the culture of architecture and urban design in Europe.

In Australia, our notion of public space is a park where you can run your English horse or walk your English hound—antiquated, borrowed ideas. Sydney didn't even have a civic space until Martin Plaza in the late '60s. Open spaces seem to make us nervous and we clog them up with ridiculous street furniture and flower stands. We have a notion that the city is only a place for work; it's open from nine to five and after that, it has about as much action as a photograph. Where are the laundrettes and supermarkets in our capital cities?

It's not like that in Italy. There are modern parts of Italian cities—air-conditioned offices and car parks—but in the older parts, business is going on, stores are open, and people live there, right in the city itself. I live as close as I can get to the heart of Sydney while still having all the amenities of living well. I'm right on the fringe—I've got amenities and stores in the immediate neighbourhood. There are more people on my street at three in the morning than three in the afternoon.

I live in Australia like a European. I'm set up for it. I've got the best of both worlds—quality of life. **99**

In tune
with Vienna

HARRY SEIDLER
Architect

"I was born in Vienna, and lived there until I was fifteen years old when, in 1938, Hitler marched in and we took our leave. When you're born in a place you retain a relationship with it which remains indelible. I go back frequently now because I am building my biggest-ever project there and I find that I'm so familiar with the place. As a teenager on your bike, you come to know every cobblestone in every street. And I find that it's one of those places that doesn't ever really change.

Vienna is the old capital city of the Austrian-Hungarian Empire and it has an incredible history. It used to be an enormous empire, all the way from the Veneto in Italy to Russia. Then there are its great museums, opera and theatre. And, of course, the most impressive public buildings almost anywhere in the world. These edifices of a great capital are monumental artworks and many—such as the Opera, Parliament, Rathaus and the Kunsthistoriche Museum—have been there since the nineteenth century. Although Austria is now tiny in comparison to its one-time empire, that part of it, that sense of grandeur, hasn't changed.

The 1930s were very, very difficult times for Europe. It was the Depression and there was endemic unemployment. That's the reason Hitler was able to gain so much power. He knew where the weaknesses lay; he promised people what they didn't have—bread and jobs. People were so desperate and they didn't realise what they were letting themselves in for.

So as a boy, I experienced Austria as a very poor country. It had a very astute, rigid kind of community. It was a place that to me meant you had to be on your toes all the time. I had an ambitious mother and from the earliest days she insisted that both my brother and I went to a high school that was quite some distance away from where we lived. She said, 'All the famous people of Vienna went to that high school and you shall go there.' I hated it. You had to click your heels, bow your head. If you got a bad mark, you had to do special additional work. There were written exams every few weeks.

It was rigid and very unfriendly, you were literally whipped into performing and, boy, did you learn! A bad mark meant learning ten verses of Homer by heart, to be recited in front of the class. It doesn't sound like a very progressive kind of education but there's something in it that makes people achieve. To this day, I can recite Homer, as can my old schoolmates. They're retired gentlemen now, but at dinner parties they still chime in with the verses!

At that time, the city was much shabbier than it is now. The magnificent buildings were all black and stained. The aristocracy used to build themselves sumptuous palaces in the middle of the city and we used to play in a park adjacent to one, Liechtenstein Palais. I remember this huge, looming building with all the shutters closed like a big black box. It's now a museum, all painted white, with a collection of priceless artworks and frescoes on the ceilings and staircases.

Although the buildings were shabby then, now they look as though they were built yesterday. Austria has become a wealthy country; it has very few raw materials but, technologically, it's very advanced. The current population is only around seven million, which is much the same as it was when I was a kid.

The underground system in Vienna is fabulous; it was one of the earliest in the world and it has now been further extended. There's a train every two and a half minutes and the stations are all polished granite. The trains are so spotless, you could eat off the carriage floor. It's a fairly confined city and the tradition has always been that people live close together which makes it a very lively place, day and night. The whole centre of the old city has been totally given over to pedestrians, there are no cars, which is wonderful. People live near the heart of things and there are so many restaurants and, of course, coffee houses. Viennese have a passion for pastries such as Mohnstrudel, always served with *Schlag*—whipped cream—and there are dozens of varieties of coffee.

Ever since the 1920s, the city of Vienna has had what's loosely termed a socialist government and it's built very avant-garde housing. Vienna is famous for its socialised housing system which has been done much better than anywhere else in Europe. Sixty-five per cent of the population lives in such housing—the city owns 200,000 apartments which are only for rent—and the standard is remarkably high.

Now, the government is looking to build progressive new housing, buildings that would be descended from what had been built in the 1920s and '30s. When I went to Vienna to receive the Gold Medal of the City [bestowed on citizens who have become recognised for work elsewhere in the world], I was asked to be involved in a project. So now I'm building the biggest thing I've ever done: housing right on the edge of the Danube, 850 apartments, some offices and an entertainment centre. It's enormous, half-a-kilometre long; I've set up an office in Vienna and would love to do more work there. My wife and I are going to have one of the apartments in the development so there's somewhere to call home when we're there, rather than living out of a suitcase.

One thing about Vienna that really earns my respect is the way art and artists are treated. There are huge works of art in public housing and in civic spaces. The Viennese culture is strongly dedicated to supporting the arts. Any day of the week there are 37 live theatre performances, which is amazing in a city smaller than Sydney. And, of course, there is an incomparable respect for design and for architecture.

The Austrian character is very autocratic. It puts its faith in education and historic precedence of excellence. Austrians aim very, very high to be the best the world can produce in the public arena. Politicians support artworks and directly commission, for instance, architects or artists, from anywhere in the world, because of their excellence in the international arena. Everyone is conscious of the importance of the arts.

I returned to Vienna for the first time in 1955. It was much poorer than it had been. It had only recently become independent again. Until 1954, Austria was occupied by the four victor nations: the Russians, the English, the French, and the Americans. So when I went back, it hadn't really got back on its feet yet. It was damaged in parts and there were gaps in the buildings, although it wasn't as badly hit as many other European cities. The first building they restored was the Opera House. A taxi driver told me this as I arrived so I asked him why they had made that choice. He replied, 'Vienna *is* the Opera House.' He said that even though he never went to the opera himself. He was so proud, and that's a very typical Viennese attitude.

The countryside in Austria is marvellous, too. You can drive just two hours from Vienna and be among the most magnificent mountain landscapes. They're unchanged because the population hasn't increased and neither have demands on the land. Conservation policies are so automatic in Austria that there's never any need to debate—no one ever talks about 'heritage' because it is all around.

Each year, during the long summer school holidays, from June to September, my mother would take us somewhere different. Sometimes we'd go to more than one country—Italy and Yugoslavia, for example. Austria is very accessible. In the winter, we'd go skiing almost every weekend. From Vienna, all I had to do was catch a tram to the edge of the city and the ski slopes would be right there. We'd also go skating. The housing blocks in Vienna are five or six storeys tall and they all have big courtyards which get covered by a layer of ice in winter and people skate on them. I was on our site at the edge of the Danube recently, and it was so cold that the river was frozen and people were skating on it. It was an incredible sight, like a Brueghel painting, with people all dark and bundled up in their woolly clothes on this white plain. There were even parents skating around, pushing prams.

Vienna is full of small moments of visual pleasure just like that. What I am really looking forward to is the completion of my life's cycle, back to my hometown, living part of the time in my project on the Danube. **99**

A year in
Florence

MARY ROSSI
Businesswoman

'Come back! I love you!' The booming voice of Theo Rossi, in 1948, ignoring the hundreds of emotional relatives and friends at Circular Quay farewelling passengers aboard the P&O liner *Orantes*, setting sail for England. They were addressed to a self-conscious me on the top deck hoping to fulfil the dream of most Australian girls of my vintage: to go abroad.

It was not to be. Defeated by a bombardment of Marconigrams, I disembarked in Adelaide, returned to Sydney and married him.

A decade later, he took me to see what I had missed. Nowhere disappointed but no place filled me with such moments of sheer delight as waking up in our large bedroom in the Palace of Tornabuoni Beacci, converted into a three-star pensione on Via Tornabuoni, Florence's most elegant street. I could never have imagined that 40 years on, I would be directing Australians to this very establishment.

It was during that visit to Florence I conceived a passion to have a real Italian experience. A year's stay—a time for me to indulge in the historical interests my studies of the Renaissance at university had awakened, a time to teach my children, who had an Italian name, an appreciation of, and pride in, their Italian heritage.

Theo's grandparents had arrived in Australia in the 1870s from northern Italy, settling in the far west of New South Wales and becoming very dinky-di Aussies. His parents were somewhat bemused that this daughter-in-law of theirs, with an English-Irish background, was intent on re-establishing contact with the land of their forebears. At the time, this was not the fashionable thing to do that it is today. In those post-War years, there was a certain stigma attached to being Italian.

In hindsight, I can't imagine how I was able to convince Theo to agree. Beset with the expenses entailed in raising eight children, I remember tabling a mathematical equation that put renting our Sydney home and sacrificing some needed building extensions on the credit side. Such rationalisation prevailed, leaving the logistical challenge of moving the whole kit and caboodle.

During the years I compered the TV program *Woman's World* for the ABC, I had met Fiamma Ferragamo of Florence. We started a friendship that has lasted a lifetime. She foresaw no problem in renting a suitable home for us—'villa' was not the 'in' word at that time—and advised that the ancestral home of Niccolo Machiavelli, author of *The Prince*, was available, close to the Piazzale Michelangelo, shops, schools and a two-minute bus ride into the centre of Florence.

November 1964 was our departure date. Tim, then aged fourteen, was despatched ahead to boarding school in England. This time with six children, I was at last to board that P&O liner to London. Theo, in order to save the five-week voyage, went by air. Baby Danielle, aged two, joined us later in Italy accompanied by a stewardess—a fact which was later to be greeted with disbelief at Florentine dinner parties.

The Sydney car was replaced by a micro-bus bought in Paris and we were each restricted to one standard 27-inch suitcase. Two steamer trunks were forwarded ahead by rail to Florence to await our arrival. This took place on a cold January day. A cap of snow covered Brunelleschi's dome on the Duomo cathedral. We drove to the address given by Fiamma and noted the grand iron gates but failed to establish the significance of the crown atop the entrance. Inside the gates was a charming little villa. 'Isn't it wonderful?' I said to Theo. It turned out this was the gatehouse!

Machiavelli's villa sat atop a hill surrounded by ten acres of gardens and orchards. It was a heritage building owned by his descendant, the Marchese Rangoni Machiavelli. Filled with antique furniture and ancestral portraits, it reminded me how I had fallen in love with the parquet floors, rich carpets and mellow colours in the Pensione Tornabuoni Beacci. Now I could revel in the glow of that wonderful patina of age in my own Florentine villa. Fiamma Ferragamo had filled the rooms with tulips—to this day, those flowers remind me of Florence. She'd also paid tremendous care to the needs of our children, right down to providing desks for their homework. Theo spent the first few days in Florence making the house as childproof as possible—including removing the Chinoiserie vase from the grand piano!

On re-reading my Italian *calendario* of this period, I can see how difficult it was at first to negotiate the ins and outs of daily Italian life. My first activity was to make contact with the local stores in the village at the end of our street. There was the pasta shop with its myriad varieties produced fresh twice a day; the cheese shop, again with varieties unknown in suburban Australia, such as fresh pecorino and ricotto. But it was at the butcher's I was stumped. Outside of the easily recognisable but far too expensive *Bistecca alla Fiorentina*, the other cuts of meat were a divine mystery. The apparently simple job of tracking down salt took weeks—I finally located it at the *tabacchi*, along with other essentials like stamps and special coins for use in public phones.

An ad in the local newspaper for a cleaner-cum-cook-cum-nanny introduced us to Maria Becattini, and my domestic dilemmas were promptly eased.

Schooling was our next project. In Europe, the term resumes in mid-January. Tim was to return to England; Virginia, aged 17, took up Italian studies in the Universita per Stranieri. As a result of this sojourn, she speaks Italian with a delightfully pure accent and—as a means of survival, I suspect, in light of her mother's poor attempts—learnt to cook many dishes, including a delicious *petti di pollo.*

Four Rossis of school age were enrolled at St Michael's Episcopal International School. Until June, they enjoyed a stimulating educational experience that involved field excursions to the Uffizi Gallery, to San Miniato al Monte, the Palazzo Vecchio, the Galleria dell'Accademia—to name just a few! Every afternoon on their way home from school, they strolled past the replica of Michelangelo's David in the Piazza della Signoria. Soon after we returned to Sydney, David Jones staged an Italian week with a David statue taking pride of place. A fig leaf had been discreetly placed to avoid upsetting lady shoppers. Sally Rossi, who was only eight or nine at the time, was extremely upset at the rather prurient remarks she'd overheard concerning the statue. This was her beloved David, at whose feet she had eaten her afternoon *gelato*!

The children's knowledge of the Italian language was not greatly enhanced by our stay in Florence. At an international school, English is mainly spoken, but Claudia, our third daughter, has retained a remarkable vocabulary which has stood us in good stead in many a tricky confrontational negotiation. As for the others, they can sing the national anthem—or belt it out, I should say!

Fiamma introduced us to a kindergarten run by her friend,

Maria Borgia—a family name not to be considered lightly, considering Lucrezia Borgia's penchant for poisoning during the Renaissance. Theo would make endless jokes on this theme while preparing Philip's lunches! Four-year-old Philip was to acquire a unique talent at Maria Borgia's. Within weeks, he could bend and kiss your hand, very gracefully, like a small cavalier.

As life settled into a regular tempo, we developed certain rituals that embellished the routines. After Sunday Mass at the Duomo, we would collect our midday meal from a local *rosticceria*: a plate of bruschetta as starters, another of spit-roasted chicken and potatoes; other indulgences included snacks of a custard-filled brioche and delicious coffee. Harry's Bar on the Lungarno for an important celebration or down the stairs to Buca Mario for a less expensive flutter.

We walked the lanes behind our home on the Via della Campora past the now-familiar crowns atop the iron gate that led to homes still bearing names of ancient Florentine families. Pencil pines, olive trees and soft sage valleys stretched behind us on one side and, on the other, the city of Florence with its terracotta roofs, spires and grand domes.

I recall weekend trips to Lucca, Venice, San Gimignano and to Rome—for Morris West's fiftieth birthday.

With spring and the appearance of apple blossoms in our orchard came the rich entertainment of Florence's Maggio Musicale festival: ballet in the Boboli Gardens, the magic of Fonteyn and Nureyev in that setting dancing Romeo and Juliet contrasted with the sombre solemnity of a Bach recital in the 13th-century gothic church of Santa Croce.

I know it's not an original thought, and E.M. Forster has written beautifully of this notion, but for those of us who have this passion for Italy, it's not just the land, but the people. For me, it's definitely the people I met in our day-to-day activities I can still see vividly. The gnarled and gentle gardener who tended the orchard and gently administered to a sick Danielle after she had unwisely gorged herself at his cherry tree. The man who parked the Rossi family bus at the Lungarno and who greeted me, twenty years later, with a cheery '*Buon giorno*, Signora Rossi', as if I'd been away a week.

But the loveliest memory of our sojourn in Florence is daughter Emma Rossi, child number nine. Conceived there, but born after we returned home, she looked like a della Robbia angel. Living proof of the belief that pregnant women who looked upon beauty would have a beautiful child!

Now she's a beautiful young woman, and two years ago she arranged with Fiamma, her godmother, a celebration in Florence with all the other Rossi children gathered there for my seventieth birthday. A day of enormous happiness and fulfilment for me in the city I so love. **"**

La dolce vita

DAIZY GEDEON
Filmmaker

"I don't remember boarding the plane bound for Sydney; I was only five at the time, but in later years I was told how my mother, sister, brother and I said goodbye to our relatives who had come to see us off at Beirut International Airport. My father was already in Australia; he had come about nine months earlier to get a job and find us a place to live so we would have somewhere to go when we arrived.

It was 1970 and the Liberal Party's reign over Australia was nearing its end. Although the racial overtones of the White Australia Policy were still prevalent, the country was experiencing a migration boom. In Lebanon, the situation had become quite tenuous. It was evident that the regional forces and the superpowers were manoeuvring for some kind of military struggle in the Middle East—and Lebanon was to be their battleground.

My father, an airline employee, was caught in the Israeli raid on Beirut Airport in 1968 when, literally out of the blue, fighter planes began shelling the airport, destroying twelve Middle East Airlines jumbos. Dad survived but swore he would take his family away from what he feared was to befall the country. Two years later he did.

In 1988, when I was twenty-three, under pressure from my mother to visit my relatives, I reluctantly agreed to return to the country of my birth. Everything I'd read about Lebanon or seen on TV suggested warmongering, poverty and terrorism. I was cautious about what I would find and what type of people my relatives would be but I wasn't scared about entering a war zone and was bemused by the fact that the plane had to dodge the craters that littered Beirut's runway. But during the flight from Paris, I looked out the window and saw such beautiful scenery that I asked the passenger next to me what country we were flying over, and when he told me it was Lebanon, my heart just went out to it. It was stunning.

That long blue hilly coastline, with buildings rising up and along it. It looked very similar to the scenery around Monaco and Monte Carlo. The mountains start to form in terraces half a kilometre in from the water. It was late October but the peaks were frosted with snow. I was expecting something drier, flatter, even desolate. When you see something so aesthetically pleasing and inviting, a barrier immediately comes down, you feel more receptive.

As we got closer to the airport, we flew over shanty towns and refugee camps and the main road from the terminal was like a wasteland. I particularly remember that advertising posters of the Marlboro Man were full of bullet holes!

From a distance, I'd had that image of intense beauty but it was different up close. I wasn't shocked because that's what I'd been expecting. Driving around the infamous Greenline that divided Beirut during the war, and seeing the devastation caused by artillery and gunfire, I felt a real sense of loss. Street after street of some of the world's most beautiful architecture had been destroyed. Looking at the hollow facades and crumbled colonnades of those stone buildings, I imagined their earlier magnificence and immediately understood why Beirut had once been known as the Paris of the East. Many international films were shot there in the 1960s—even James Bond movies—because of the scenery and the architecture; I saw a documentary on SBS TV recently called *Lebanon Bits and Pieces* which was amazing because it showed scenes from all these big movies shot there with stars such as Brigitte Bardot, Mickey Rooney and David Niven.

Despite the bombing that punctuated the otherwise calm nights I spent in Beirut, I felt strangely at peace, really connected with this crazy city and its wild but warm people. The Lebanese are very friendly and they also have a great sense of humour. They're generous, and ethical and moral in many respects because it's such a religious country. They are very sophisticated and cosmopolitan, too; Lebanon has long been the centre for liberal intellectual thought in the Middle East.

And there's a real sense of community. If you're having a party, for example, the whole apartment block will come and help you prepare the food, clean up afterwards. If you're sick, or a family member passes away, everyone will be there for you. I think the fact Lebanon has been at war for so long has made a definite contribution to the way the Lebanese think. They've seen so many people around them being killed and they really live life to the limit—there's this entrenched feeling that it could change at any time.

It's also something to do with the Mediterranean lifestyle— Italians, Greeks and people along the Riviera have that same sensual attitude. They party late into the evening, enjoying *la dolce vita* to the hilt. But they also work very hard. Maybe it's the climate, but they get up at, say, seven, go to work by eight, then finish at two, have their lunch, maybe a siesta, then work a few more hours in the afternoon. Work days aren't programmed as they are in Australia but productivity is high.

Having the main meal at lunchtime, followed by a very light dinner, makes a difference to the way the day is structured. Or, if they're going out to dinner they'll wait until very late, especially in the summer.

My relatives wanted to take me everywhere but I also explored alone. Hitchhiking is illegal, but if you're walking along the street, motorists beep and ask if you want a lift. I have an Australian accent when I speak Lebanese so it was obvious I was a tourist but most people know English and it's very easy to communicate.

In the evenings, my cousins took me to nightclubs and bars brimming with people out for a good time. The Lebanese love music and dancing—belly dancing, in particular—and the clubs where the dancers perform are incredibly plush, especially up at Broumana in the hills, overlooking Beirut and the Mediterranean. The restaurants there are set in gardens, with twinkling lights all around.

All the great international designers have shops in Beirut—they were there even during the war—and the Kazlik is a really exclusive shopping area, just like Double Bay in Sydney. There's definitely a rich élite, people really like to look good, and they want to have big houses. The thing to do is have a home in Beirut—often it'll be a big, old apartment—and a villa in the country plus a summer chalet at the beach or in the mountains. All this requires a lot of servants—Russian domestic workers are apparently all the go at the moment. Families always go out together, very noisy and very social.

My first visit to Lebanon lasted six weeks, even though I'd intended to stay just a fortnight. It turned into a voyage of self-discovery. I toured the east, west and north of the country. Lebanon's surprisingly small and you can drive from one end to the other in a day, or travel across in just a few hours. You have to drive carefully in the mountains, though, because there are no guard rails or barriers on the roads, but the scenery is exquisite. It's not particularly forested but there are cedars, of course, for which Lebanon is famous, and some of these are hundreds of years old with very wide trunks. Many were chopped down during the war but there's a movement to revitalise the forests and a lot of replanting is taking place.

Tourists don't associate Lebanon with skiing but you can drive up to the mountains outside Beirut and go for a ski in the morning and be back by mid-afternoon for a swim in the sea. My friends there often drive to the skifields in the wee hours, have a huge breakfast and be out skiing just after sunrise, then come back to the city for a siesta. Or they'll be up all night and then decide to have a snack at, say, three in the morning, so it's off to a café for a Lebanese-style pizza with olives and cheese and a delicious oregano paste called *zahtar*.

On that visit in 1988, I saw Roman ruins most tourists have never even heard about. I walked along white-sand beaches right in Beirut overlooked by million-dollar apartments which are almost too luxurious to be true. I saw where Jesus Christ turned water into wine at the marriage of Cana and I sipped on fine local wine from Chataura Vineyard—it produces a red which is rated among the top ten in the world—as I gazed at the blueness of the Mediterranean.

I knew I was part of Lebanon's history and for the first time in my life I felt a sense of belonging to some thing, some place, some time and people. I embraced my past and the origins of my ancestors. When I'd been a young child, in Sydney, I'd been ashamed of being Lebanese, of being different, a wog. Now I felt proud of Lebanon and its resilient people who had overcome the attempts of occupation and annexations by other armies. And I was proud that through it all, the humility of the people had not been destroyed.

I returned to Australia filled with a sense of purpose, determined to open the eyes of the rest of the world to the truth of Lebanon. I wanted to share my experience with others who may have been struggling with the same identity issues and to explain how for me it was no longer a question of: Am I Lebanese or am I Australian? I knew I could be both, there was no longer a need to choose between the two.

I've been back ten times since, each visit finding out something more about my roots. After the first visit, when I realised I could contribute to what was happening in Lebanon, I became very interested in the dynamics of the war, and I moved away from sports writing into features and current affairs, and I went back to university to study Middle Eastern politics and history, and international relations, so I could put it all into an understandable context.

I definitely thought there was a film of some sort to be made there. My next visit was a year later. I went to do an interview with General Michel Aoun, who was the head of the country at the time, and a couple of other leaders, and I spent ten days there. That visit was particularly interesting because Beirut Airport had been bombed so I had to go through Cyprus and catch an overnight ferry. You arrive into the port of Jounieh, about 30 kilometres north of Beirut, at dawn, the birds are singing and everything looks sleepy and almost ancient, like you've travelled back to an earlier time. You can still catch a ferry or hydrofoil from Cyprus to Lebanon. It takes about seven hours, although some vessels are faster. You can get a cabin or you can stay on deck and make a real night of it, with cabarets, casinos and belly dancers going all night on some ferries. The experience is very similar to catching a ferry across from Brindisi in Italy to the Greek Islands, and the climate and atmosphere are equally great.

On my first trip, there were bombs; on my second visit, I visited the front line. I didn't feel scared, but I fully realised the danger. I felt very Lebanese and patriotic then, because the war was between the Syrians—who were trying to take over Lebanon—and the Lebanese army.

On later visits, I discovered what rural village life is like. It's almost like living in the country here in Australia but it's much more concentrated because the houses are very close together, clustered around beautiful green waterholes. It's not unlike Spain and Italy—terracotta roof tiles, flowering vines, cobblestoned streets, colours of clay and ochre. Lebanon has a hot climate so some areas are very dry, but most of the country is very fertile with some regions producing wonderful fruit and vegetables, and olives, mostly green, but black as well. The Bekaa Valley is amazingly lush; in the years of Jesus Christ when Rome occupied Lebanon, the Bekaa was known as the granary of the Roman Empire because the food produced from this valley literally fed the whole empire. Now everything is grown there—oranges, grapefruit, apples, wheat, grapes, mangoes, cherries and strawberries. The fruit is *so* big and grown without chemicals. People in Lebanon live to a great age because the diet is so healthy.

Lebanon is the only country in the Middle East overflowing with fresh water. In the political Middle East, they believe the biggest crisis is the water situation, and the next major war is going to be over water, because the Arab world doesn't have melting mountain streams. In the Bekaa Valley, you can go to this very dusty, arid spot and there's a restaurant in the middle of nowhere, beside an ice-cold river, flowing strongly. You can pick your fresh fish and it's cooked for you. Little kids play in the river, jumping in and out of big rubber wheels.

Outside the cities, the landscape is biblical, with donkeys and goats everywhere. Once you get into the villages, there are old men wearing Turkish hats, because the Turks were in Lebanon for 400 years, until early this century. And they're dressed in drawstring pants, with white shirts. For tourists, it's a wonderful place—all that history and scenery, and it's very affordable.

It was after seeing and experiencing all this history and culture on my numerous trips to Lebanon that I began to question the accuracy of the media and to reassess who I was. The problems I faced coming to terms with my identity are no different from those of immigrants around the world. We have all experienced feelings of dislocation, unfamiliar territory and discrimination in one form or another, so we have all asked ourselves the same questions about our origins and purpose. Which makes it difficult to understand why stereotypical perceptions in the Western media about peoples of other countries still persist—and that is definitely the case with Lebanon, its people constantly portrayed as being barbaric and illiterate. You're never given the complete story.

I decided to make a documentary focusing on my personal experiences with identity and ethnicity. Reclaiming my heritage has enabled me to embrace my past, present and future. I had to sell my house to make *Lebanon . . . Imprisoned Splendour* and it took enormous determination and perseverance to persuade Omar Sharif to be part of the project. He had grown up in Egypt but his family came from Lebanon and he was heartbroken that the war had almost destroyed what he called the most beautiful country on earth. He was inspirational to work with and I'd decided I would pay him whatever he asked, no matter how I had to raise the money. In the end, he wouldn't take a cent. He said he believed in what I was doing—and he wanted me to get my house back! **99**

A fish out
of water

TETSUYA WAKUDA
Chef

"I come from a town called Hamamatsu in Shizuoka Prefecture, Japan, which is on the main island of Honshu, between Tokyo and Osaka. I was twenty-two when I finished my schooling and before getting a job I decided to go overseas. I wanted to experience other countries—and not just to visit, but to live. Just for a year, or so I thought. I could speak only Japanese—hardly any English at all, and I couldn't understand the Australian accent—but somehow [in Sydney], I managed to meet all sorts of people.

The day I arrived in Sydney—the second of May, 1982—I asked the taxi driver to take me to the centre of the city. You know where he took me? Taylor Square. And I thought, this is not what I expected. Where are the beaches and kangaroos and koalas? There were old drunks sitting in the park—very strange. I went to an estate agent to find somewhere to live and he was to become my friend.

This real estate agent found me a job peeling potatoes and washing dishes at Fishwives Restaurant, which was then in Surry Hills, but I was very lucky to be introduced to [Sydney chef] Tony Bilson, who asked me if I could make basic Japanese dishes and I said I could, so he gave me a job at Kinselas and that's how my cooking career began. For Neville Wran's birthday, Tony told me to do something 'soupy' so I made a sort of Japanese bouillabaisse. I often had to pinch myself to believe I was working overseas, making money, speaking English, cooking for celebrities. It felt much more like home than Japan ever had.

The attraction for Australia was instant and I never got homesick, either. Ever since I arrived fifteen years ago, I've felt happier here than in Japan.

When I first got to Sydney, I had nothing—hardly any money, just one small bag, because I wasn't sure if I would stay. My parents were convinced I'd be straight back; my mother told me I'd never survive. When I was a child in Hamamatsu, I saw programs about Australia, and then at school, when I was about thirteen or fourteen years old, I learned about the White Australia policy. I thought, well, if only white people are allowed to live there, it must be a very special place!

Then I saw Australia on various TV documentaries, and became fascinated by it—its size, in particular. I spent a lot of time watching documentaries when I was a child. My favourite program was Kaoru Kanataka's *Around the World*, which must have run for more than 20 years. She was very popular and I grew up with that show as part of my Sunday morning ritual.

I was an independent boy. Both my parents worked in our fabric factory and apart from watching TV, I spent a lot of time reading books and learning about the world. I became fascinated by all things foreign. Whenever I saw a *gaijin*, a foreigner, in Hamamatsu, I would stare at them—blond hair, blue eyes, so different—and I'd always hope they'd ask me the way to the station! I remember saying to my mother, 'I wouldn't mind being one of those people.' She looked at me in horror and asked if I'd lost my mind. We have an expression in Japan: *mizu eta sakana*, which means, 'like a fish out of water'. That was me, even back then.

I studied and practised English as much as I could. Our

house was traditional, with sliding shoji screens, but in my bedroom I had everything in Western style: timber floors, a bed instead of a futon on the floor. For breakfast, I'd eat typical Japanese food—rice, miso soup, grilled fish—but I'd have toast and cereal as well. Subconsciously, I must have been preparing for a new future outside Japan.

Nobody else in my family has ever left Japan. For the first ten years after I came to Australia, I didn't go back at all to see my parents. And they haven't been to visit me. All my other relatives have, but not my parents. They are very conservative, like most Japanese of their generation, and because I'm their only son, I think they are expecting me to go to Hamamatsu and pick them up and bring them here. I tell them they're healthy enough, and if they want to come over here, then they should just do it. That's the Australian way.

When I went back to Japan after that first ten-year break, things were much more industrialised. Hamamatsu was no longer a country town—it was more like a modern city, with signs for Honda, Suzuki and Yamaha and, of course, air pollution. I felt nothing in my heart so I told my parents, 'This is not my home town.' I'll have family ties with that place as long as my parents are alive but I'm an Aussie now.

There are things I miss, of course. Like the food, the hospitality and the details you find, especially in fine restaurants. The best places to dine may be incredibly small—between six and twelve seats. You'd never find that in Australia. For example, in Osaka there's a tiny restaurant called Kahara with eight counter seats. There are no waiters: the chef knows exactly when to serve you because he's watching so carefully. Everything is beautifully presented on individually designed ceramic dishes. It's Japanese food but there's a special twist to it and, in summer, they keep the chopsticks overnight in the fridge so the food doesn't stick to them. You wouldn't encounter that sort of attention anywhere else in the world.

I was very lucky to get into Kahara. A customer of mine took me because I've talked about opening a restaurant just like that—almost a private one—and he wanted me to see it. There is another small restaurant which is similar, in Tokyo, also an eight-seater, but I haven't been there yet. It's booked out for the next ten years, because there are only two tables, for four people each. A friend of mine has a permanent booking, for as long as the restaurant exists, the first Tuesday of every month. Basically, unless someone on the regular reservations list dies, you'll never get a table. No one ever cancels, because if for some reason you can't go, you pass on the booking to a friend. Pretty hard for an outsider to get in, but my friend has promised to take me there next time I'm in Tokyo. Dinner in a restaurant like that would cost between $200 and $300 per head. And then, drinks are expensive— any good restaurant in Japan you go to, you'll be charged very heavily. A mark-up of 400 or 500 per cent is not unusual.

Even as a boy, I loved food. My mother is a very good cook but because my parents were both working, I would eat out a lot. When I came home from school, there'd be no afternoon tea waiting, but my mother would leave me money and I could go and buy something, so I discovered all sorts of food and places to eat. On weekends, the family often ate out, too. I loved sushi and Korean barbecue—I still do. But it wasn't just what we ate when we went to restaurants—it was the event, watching other people, the sense of theatre.

I used to like visiting my mother's parents in Sendai, which is known for its hot springs. The countryside is very pretty, and where my grandparents lived was like a fishing village. Some mornings we'd go and watch the fishermen bring in their catch and I loved that—I knew we'd be having fresh fish for breakfast. In Hamamatsu, I used to go out on my uncle's boat on Lake Hamana and we'd catch whiting, a local fish called *haze*, little jewfish, snapper and bream. My mother would cook them—sometimes with tempura batter, or just fried or grilled. These days the lake is polluted, but then it was clean and the fish were delicious.

Now, when I go back to Japan, I try to sample the food from different regions. The cuisine in Sapporo [capital of the northernmost island of Hokkaido] is particularly good. When I'm there, I realise, too, that I miss the pattern of the seasons, the real definition between summer and winter. Although I certainly don't long for the harsh Japanese winter. I'm much happier with Australia's mild climate. In Sydney, I have a cabin cruiser and I can go out on the harbour year-round. I do a bit of fishing on it but it never matters if I catch something or not. It's the peace, the incredible beauty, and that sense of being alone—you can't experience that in Japan.

I feel more at ease with Australian people than with Japanese people. I find the Japanese too formal, and also I don't like the rituals of the language, the indirect way of talking. In Australia, people get straight to the point, they don't waste your time. Everything's black or white. It's never like that in Japan and I get very irritated, especially when doing business there. In a way, I suppose I've broken the cord with Japan— I've become a *gaijin*, just like those foreigners I used to see in Hamamatsu when I was a schoolboy!

I'm on Japanese TV doing food programs quite a bit— newsy stuff, educating people. My parents sometimes get upset about not seeing me and tell their friends they don't have a son any more but, there I am, on their TV set. They do have a son—it's just that he's an Aussie. 🙶

Chapter 5

THE LOVE OF FOOD

Travel as a
culinary journey

Cook's
tours

STEPHANIE ALEXANDER
Chef

"In 1949, when I was nine, my parents bought sixty acres of bushland at the back of Rosebud on Victoria's Mornington Peninsula. In those days it was very wild and rural. Until it was sold, in 1965, it was always a place to which I returned with enormous pleasure. Driving from the city, I would reach Dromana and just know I was heading home. I could sail down the highway and turn off and be in a little oasis that was green and gorgeous and full of good conversation and great food.

I also loved the foreshore, particularly in winter when it was deserted. The Rosebud foreshore is very sheltered and grass grows tall between huge tea-trees. As children, we would ride our bicycles along this amazing strip, weaving among the tea-tree branches. It was so green and lovely. On hot days we would drop our bikes and go for a swim.

Nowadays, people write snide articles about the foreshore campers but it's really quite unfair. There are many families whose lives have meshed with other families at Rosebud. They keep returning to the same place every year—it's extraordinary. The coastal areas of Rye, Tootgarook and Blairgowrie, which are less fashionable and have fewer campsites, are incredibly beautiful.

When we were children, my mother would say, 'If this were Europe there would be a tea-tree festival and a flathead festival every year.' It's true even today, and she realised that thirty years ago. The flathead is an exquisite fish, and in those days it was caught in incredible profusion in Port Phillip Bay. My father would bring home three or four dozen flathead after only an hour and a half. We had huge amounts of fish, which my mother had to find ways of using. We would have little flathead tails crispy fried for breakfast, and minced up fish balls served with sauce, or as an appetiser.

Trying to find ways to use the fish prompted my mother's remark. In Europe, this phenomenon would be a major tourist attraction. People would flock to the beaches where every little kiosk would sell flathead in some way. My mother's attitude was that this great resource should be celebrated. It's an attitude I share and wherever I go, I'm always looking. The potential is always there for something absolutely marvellous.

My mother found it necessary to have things around her that grew and waved in the wind and looked beautiful. She needed to have things she could pull out of the soil or pick from a tree. The garden she created provided all of this. It was a very big garden, full of tea-trees and banksias, and was largely wild. From the house my father built, we could see trees out of every window and her garden was in amongst them. It was very Edna Walling in style, naturalising little pockets of this and that in the existing landscape. An old creek gully ran through the property and was cool and lush and, of course, there was a birdbath. Wonderful wattle birds would come to the kitchen window where the sun lit up the pink-gold bracts of the unpruned abelia bushes. As a child, I was unconsciously absorbing my mother's love of plants and natural environments.

Being at Greenslopes was always a very centring experience. It was a place of security and incredible beauty. Whenever I returned, it was for the whole package—the beautiful environment, family life, lovely food and good conversation. Essentially, that place has been a touchstone for me forever.

My friends have felt it, too, and enjoyed the expansive hospitality and the sometimes radical philosophy.

Now I respond to those same attributes wherever I travel. The natural landscape of a place is just as important to me as the food. I will always respond to beautiful, natural scenery. As much as I might have enjoyed a fantastic lunch at a country restaurant, I am just as likely to remember the river or the trees. I will remember a lovely picnic spot just as well as what we ate.

I love losing myself on tiny, minor roads. You can do that very quickly in France. I've always responded to the lushness of the French countryside, and while driving there I have sometimes been overwhelmed by its beauty.

I have strong pulls toward the Perigord and Dordogne regions, in the south-west of France, because I just find them so deep and green. There are huge forests and some of the valleys seem completely untouched and unpeopled. That obviously isn't true, but you can drive through mountains and valleys and see only a couple of buildings and pass very few cars. Perigord is incredibly beautiful so you don't need a particular reason to be there. I just wander through the medieval villages and look in amazement at architecture that hasn't changed over the centuries. I climb steep little cobbled streets, past stone fountains, and gaze in the shop windows.

I spend a lot of time enjoying the countryside, either driving or walking. Just looking at it relaxes me and lifts my spirit. As a traveller, I prefer to stay somewhere at least for a few days—to find a little centre to radiate out from. I find I need time to appreciate my surroundings, time to sniff the place and really walk about.

Country markets are an enchanting and inspirational

feature of the French countryside. There are fine markets in little towns in Perigord and I've visited wonderful ones in the towns of Perigeux and Sarlat. I find it fascinating to see how local people sell things, how they bargain in the markets, how they choose, what words they use.

I love the way local farmers will bring a very small amount of produce to market. Often it is cheese in various stages of drippiness, depending on whether it is a day, or a week, or ten days old. A stall might only have fifteen cheeses supplemented with a few bunches of something that has been gathered or grown on the farm, sometimes wild herbs and a basket or two of gathered mushrooms.

Nowadays, one also meets stall-holders who work the markets like they do here in Australia, so you will see the olive man in one market and then again in a neighbouring village another day. In the deep countryside, though, there is still a sense that what is being brought to the weekly market has actually been produced by the stall-holder. Although it sounds like one is harking back to a life that is unsustainable, it's important to realise there are still people out there who care about producing things themselves and who have no problem finding an appreciative buyer. It says something about the population, too. In the countryside there is a sense that people care about the quality of what they eat. I find that respect endlessly renewing. In the language used in the markets, there's a sense that buying food is a life-enriching transaction.

As I love shopping in these markets, I need to have access to a kitchen. Otherwise I'm restricted to picnic lunches, which are lovely, but then only certain sorts of ingredients can be purchased. I've had quite a few picnic lunches where we've chomped on sandy radishes because I couldn't resist their pink and white stripes, but there was nowhere to wash them. On the other hand, without picnics I would never have tasted a memorable squid pie, enjoyed under the towering Mont St Victoire in Provence—so familiar from the paintings of Cézanne.

Twenty-two years ago I took a little flat in the south of France at Beaulieu-sur-Mer, which is just out of Nice. That was lovely because the old market in Nice was delightful. I haven't been back to that market for twenty years, so it could well have changed dramatically. I would go shopping and get into conversations with the butcher. The extraordinary cost of meat, compared to Australia, amazed me, but then when I saw the way in which it was trimmed, tied and seasoned, I could understand some of that price. French butchers treat meat with a great deal more respect than happens in most of our butcher shops. It is a revelation to buy meat that has been so lovingly handled and beautifully prepared.

Recently, I stayed in an Italian villa in Umbria with [Barossa Valley chef] Maggie Beer and her husband, and my two daughters and some friends. The group was all very interested in food so we shopped and talked to the shopkeepers and tried out our Italian and went to the markets. We also enjoyed visits to nearby Perugia, which is a university town. There were a lot of young people doing the *passeggiata* at night, chatting with their coats slung over their shoulders and sunglasses pushed up on their heads—lots of attitude.

Our villa was extremely remote. We were on top of a mountain ten very difficult kilometres from the nearest village. It was rutted roads all the way, first gear at five kilometres per hour. On top of our mountain, we felt utterly cut off from the world. It was wonderfully peaceful and very good for the soul. From the villa we looked out on a totally green landscape. Of course, there were other farmhouses, but we couldn't see them because they were all tucked away in their own bits of greenery.

At the bottom of the mountain, in the flatter areas, the soil was incredibly fertile. Even quite small plots were heavily planted and when we were there, in early autumn, the land seemed to be bursting with vegetables. On one occasion we walked the ten kilometres to Umbertide, our closest market town. Stalls were selling extraordinary tomatoes. They were incredibly cheap, obviously locally grown and available in great profusion. So we did a lot of things with tomatoes. We sliced them for lunch, liberally anointed with great olive oil, and we made scarlet pasta sauces.

We bought fabulous chicken, guinea fowl and squab pigeons. Another time, Maggie pot roasted butter-tender farmed rabbit. Many of our meals were cooked over the open wood-fired grill, so typical in Tuscan and Umbrian kitchens. It was wonderful being with people who all love to cook, eat and drink. We had a sense that we shared a purpose and I didn't have to worry that I wanted to spend a good bit of the day thinking about food.

Maggie and I hope to recreate that atmosphere when we take a group of people to Italy. This time we are going to a house near Siena in Tuscany. We want to encourage people to cook in a relaxed way and to better understand how to profit from what is locally available. This is what I have done many times in parts of France.

I have had delightful holidays here, there and everywhere, particularly in places where I can buy food, cook it and eat it with friends. All of them remain as little pockets of memory. I don't feel I have to rush back to these places, but I remember them all with great affection. **99**

Toujours
Sévérac

MARION HALLIGAN
Writer

"It's interesting to use this term 'love affair with France' because I think it works on all sorts of levels to call a relationship with a country a love affair. It's partly a matter of chemistry, as you get between people; you watch a couple together and you see they're immensely involved with one another, and you don't always understand quite why it is he chose her and she chose him, but then you decide it's obviously the chemistry that works. I think that to talk about having a love affair with France is really very much a matter of chemistry, too.

Paris is where everybody wants to go but it was quite accidental how I got there, because when I married Graham, a French scholar, he wanted to go back to France, because he'd already spent some years there. And by the time we went we had a baby, and this changes the way you travel, very much. If you haven't got a baby and you've got plenty of money, you can travel around, or if you haven't got plenty of money, you can do things roughly and get about, but when you've got a baby you have to go about in a certain way, and I think also you have to stay in one place for a certain amount of time. So what I tended to do was go to places in France and stay there for a while. And that really means that you get to know it.

The first time I went to France was in 1966, when the baby was very small, and people used to say then that the French were so rude. I never found them rude, because I was out there buying things with the baby in the pram and they'd talk to me about her. My French wasn't all that good, but I never found people unsympathetic about it, either.

The first trip was very brief; we'd been in Cambridge and we only really visited France, but then in 1971, when we had a five-year-old and a two-year-old, we actually spent a sabbatical year in France because friends of ours had an apartment which they said we could take over. When we went to live in this apartment in Suresnes we found that, going to market and shopping as the locals did, people were very friendly. But sometimes funny things would happen, too. I remember I wanted to buy some pâté, and I wanted a fair bit, so I asked for half a kilo and the stall-holder looked at me and said, 'That's a lot.' Then I realised people don't buy pâté like that, you buy *un morceau*, the seller will hold it up with a knife and say, this much, or whatever, so whenever I went back to that stall, the woman would have her joke, and she'd hold out her hands like somebody showing a fish and say, 'You want some pâté?' Half a kilo, of course, is a walloping lot.

Our friends' apartment turned out to be pretty hopeless for us because it was on the top floor of a house and tiny. And the kids didn't like it; they felt squashed. A friend of ours, Bernard, inherited a house in Sévérac from his grandfather's cousin, and he said we could go and live there for a month or two early in the summer. So we left Paris and that was the beginning of our love affair with Sévérac. It was a big house in this medieval village which has a castle on the top of a hill surrounded by a moat, which is now just a street, called Les Douves, or Moat Street, and there are houses actually built into the wall of the castle. The old lady who'd lived in Bernard's house had been a seamstress and her brother made furniture out of the cotton reels she emptied. So the house was full of odd furniture, very curly stuff because cotton reels are very heavily waisted. Our friend Bernard called the style Louis Bobbin, which was the local joke, like Louis Quatorze furniture.

The house was pretty much as it had been when it was built in the late 18th century. It had a fuel stove, a kind of lavatory down in the cellar—one of those holes in the ground which you pour a jug of water through. It didn't have any bathroom, and it was great fun, actually, heating the water on the fuel stove, pouring it in a basin and bathing the kids. I used to do the washing on the back doorstep, on the corner of the street, because the water splashed around so much. Just up the street there was a *lavoir*, a public washing place, and the women of the village washed their husbands' farm clothes there, and I've always thought that if I'd been braver, I might have gone up with some washing and talked to them.

This *lavoir* was built into the side of the hill, and the main street ran slightly above it, and that street was full of shops selling bathroom fittings, baths and basins and so on, and it was just the beginning of change for the village which we saw, going first in 1971 and then again a few years ago. There has been enormous change, rural people have left the old villages and though they have more comfortable lives and it's selfish of us to want the picturesque to remain, yet there was a kind of life in that picturesqueness. You'd hear this jangling in the street and you'd look out and there'd be a whole flock of Roquefort sheep going past. The shepherds would take them up and put them under the houses at night, and feed them there. The houses inside the village walls were ramshackle and kids would be falling over steps with tumbledown edges. It was full of life and energy.

Now, these houses are beautifully restored and closed most of the year. They're what the French call *résidence sécondaire*, a holiday home. When you say to French people, 'I've just been to Sévérac,' they'll ask, 'Where is it?' and you try to explain it's near the gorges of the Tarn, near Rodez, near Millau, it's ninety kilometres up from Montpelier on the coast, it's south of the Auvergne. But even if they don't know exactly where it is, they always say one eats very well in that region.

Our friend Monsieur Joyes, whose job had been connecting houses to the water supply, knew the area very well and he would take us to remote little inns, so we'd turn up and madame would say, 'Well, I really haven't got any food, I can put you something together,' and she'd bring out a whole pile of local charcuterie, then she'd do, say, an omelette with Roquefort, then perhaps some vegetables, then she'd find a pigeon or some veal. But they're very fond—or, rather, they were very fond—of two meat courses. For a tiny amount of money, compared with what meals in Australia cost, course after course would appear and wine used to be included— half a litre of the local rough red, but quite good, really.

When I first went to Sévérac, I realised you couldn't really buy vegetables in the market at all, but that's because most people grew their own. They'd buy their various poultry and so on alive, and have the legs tied together and carry them off like that. And you can still buy live poultry and trout which they'll pull out and bop on the head to sell them to you fresh. And there's great Roquefort cheese. We actually went to the village of Roquefort, which is near a place called St Affrique, and bought a whole cheese, very blue, almost black in bits, which was just great.

We got to know the local people, and one day they posted us a big chunk of Roquefort all the way to Canberra. The Whitlam government was being critical of France in the Pacific at that time and the French weren't actually speaking to the Australians. There were boycotts against mail from

France but this Roquefort finally arrived, a bit wet and juicy and totally illegal. We unwrapped it and thought, my God, and ate it. It was very good.

Quite often when we arrived in Sévérac it would be after dark, and we'd come on roads that really wound through the hills, because it's just south of the Auvergne and it's quite high up, not unlike Canberra in some ways. It's not country for cattle but the Roquefort sheep are very sure-footed, like goats. It's inhospitable terrain, which is probably why you don't get a lot of vegetables there, because it's just not fertile. But you'd be driving across this great plateau country, very like the Blue Mountains in parts, and the valleys cut down in this very steep way, only on an even larger scale.

We'd come winding across the plateau and, at the right time of year, the castle would be suddenly before us, all lit up, because the village itself would have a few lights but it wouldn't be very bright, just odd streetlights and such. But the castle would be floodlit, so you'd have this medieval edifice suspended in the air. The way I described it in my novel *Spider Cup* was that it makes you think of Jerusalem, the holy city, that appears in dreams to people, just hanging in the heavens, lit up.

One of the things we started to do when we lived in Sévérac was to drive around and look at the local architecture, which tends to be pretty old. A lot of the churches, for instance, were built in the 11th century, if not earlier. In fact I came to write *Cockles of the Heart* because we got so keen on looking at these churches, and realised that a lot of them were there because they were on the pilgrimage routes to Santiago de Compostela and that one day we should make the pilgrimage instead of just moiling around the middle.

Sometimes I think I should stop going back to France and go somewhere else but it comes down to this sort of chemistry. France is like a beloved person and there's this huge affection built up through spending 25 years going there whenever we've had the opportunity. Even though Sévérac is now a bit of a shut-down village, when we get to the house and open the door, the place always has a delicious smell, of coffee and spices in the cupboards. It never seems musty, maybe that's because of the stone walls. We open the windows and look out at this amazing valley. You can't see the castle from the house, because that's sort of behind it, but we can look over the valley to a chapel. There's still a little chinky noise of sheep-bells, because there are still Roquefort sheep there, even though people don't keep them under the house. We think, yes, we've come home. Then we begin to make plans for the places we'll drive to and have meals.

What particularly interests me about a French meal is its perfect shape. It's like a novel or a short story: it builds up, then it closes, so that you start off with some small thing, you go on to the main work, followed by a bit of cheese or fruit perhaps, dessert, then it's concluded. I think one of the very first articles I wrote about this was the idea that instead of having the Australian meal of meat and three veg and pudding, why not put one of the vegetables as the first course, a little salad of beetroot or tomato. Then there could be a salad with the main course or a handful of beans and a lamb chop, then a little piece of cheese or some fruit, and those who want puddings, can make puddings. I was, and still am, very interested in that whole idea of a meal consisting of a lot of small parts. But when I go to restaurants these days, I'll often have two entrée courses, because I don't have the eating capacity I once had, but I still like the idea of progression, of ritual, of sitting over a meal and talking about it, with a glass of wine.

I like all sorts of particularly French things which come out of thrift, out of a peasant society, out of the fact that you've got to use everything you've got, if it's edible. If you kill a pig, you use every tiny bit—you don't throw away the trotters or the ears, you even make something out of the head. Anything green in the garden, you do something with. Any fruits that are around, you turn them into something. They might be too sour, so you mix them with sugar and make some sort of jam or preserve. There's a sense that you don't waste anything.

I must confess that *andouillettes* are one of the first things I always eat when I go to France. They're tripe sausages, and when you cut into them, all these little furls of intestine curl out. They're usually eaten with mustard and chips, and sometimes they're crumbed, always golden brown. I also love those thin French steaks. They must be a cheap cut because you don't pay much for them; they come pink in the middle, and chewy but tender. I always eat them and think about Roland Barthès, who said that this is the archetypal French meal, this steak and chips that he called 'the alimentary sign of Frenchness'. And the French do those thin chips which are very naughty because you get more fat per squillimetre of chip, which is in fact very, very delicious.

Around Sévérac you get a lot of pork charcuterie. There are lark pâtés which normally I wouldn't eat but sometimes somebody gives you a tiny little tin with one inside. Presumably they don't wipe out all the larks doing it! Another great thing in the area is *brandade*, or salt cod. You can make it here; it costs a fortune to buy the salt cod but it was originally quite a cheap dish. You get this leathery piece of fish—and I've got some wonderful recipes that say, 'soak it in a running fountain or a stream for 24 hours'—and you put it through lots of changes of water, and you cream it up with mashed potato and a lot of garlic.

Aligot is the great dish of the area; it's my daughter's favourite, she makes a very good one in Australia although it's not quite the same as you get locally. It's made with a cheese called *cantal* which comes from the mountains a bit to the north of Sévérac, and it ends up a cheese with the texture of cheddar—a sort of matured, yellowy cheese—but when it's fresh and it's still a bit soft and squishy, you dice it, cube it, and put it in a pan with a lot of garlic and a whole lot of cream and a little bit of olive oil, and you stir in mashed potato. My daughter makes it with mozarella, which has that slightly rubbery texture, so when you eat it, all the cheese goes into threads. Around Sévérac it would be served on its own; you'd get a dish of *aligot*, with maybe a little trout or pigeon before it. It's rich and peasanty; if you weren't leading a peasant's life, you'd get hugely fat on *aligot*. You get wonderful strawberries around there, and then when you go from Sévérac to Millau, which is one of the two medium-big towns, about thirty or forty kilometres away, in the gorges of the Tarn, there are wonderful fig trees on the slopes. And peaches and apricots and blackcurrants. All of that makes a pretty good meal: local trout, a bit of *aligot*, maybe a porky sausagey thing, and a peach and Roquefort, a strawberry or two.

When I first got married I bought Elizabeth David's *French Provincial Cooking* and that was the book I took with me to France. I remember eating fennel in Sévérac and coming back and asking my greengrocer if he sold it. I had to tell him that it looks a bit like celery but it's more bulbous and it's got a slightly aniseedy taste—within a couple of years there was fennel all over the place. Now I think Australia has world-class food—superior to France in a lot of places. French food is still amazing, but you can have bad, overcooked food there.

Sévérac is always with me. I think about it a great deal of the time and so do my children. So far, we've not regretted going back, haven't felt it's changed so much that it's no longer itself. We add to, we don't spoil, our memories.

I first heard the sound of the nightingale in Sévérac. Bernard was drinking herb tea. He said, 'Of course you don't drink coffee at night, do you?' And I said, 'Oh, yes, it doesn't keep me awake.' Then he said, 'Doesn't it?' So he made this Parisian heart-starter coffee and I drank some. It did keep me awake all night but because I couldn't sleep, I heard a nightingale singing in the valley. You don't easily lose a memory like that. **99**

To market,
to market

CHARMAINE SOLOMON
Asian food expert

"I've really learned a lot from visiting markets around the world, especially in Asia. It's so different to walking into a glamorous department store and seeing what's imported from other places. The market is where growers come to sell their fresh produce and you see and understand what the people of the country really eat. It's always an eye-opener.

I'm constantly surprised by what I find. In Thailand I was delighted to discover a sort of Asian *bouquet garni*, which consists of lemon grass, kaffir lime leaves and galangal all tied up in a bundle ready to put into a dish and simmer. I've also found some of the most beautiful asparagus I've ever seen in the markets of Bangkok and Chiang Mai. I'd always thought of asparagus as a European vegetable but the Thais love it; they call it 'foreign bamboo shoot'.

Thai markets are very impressive. The displays are quite beautiful: there will be massive heaps of mushrooms and then, just two feet away, huge piles of exotic orchids. To the Thais, it's perfectly natural that all these things should be in the same shop, rather than having a separate market or district for flowers and another for vegetables.

At the weekend market in Bangkok, which is a huge open area, my guide indicated a man with a big black garbage bag—all lumpy, as if it were full of big potatoes—and said it contained drinking coconuts and we should try them. The outer coir part had been cut off and the nuts had been roasted in their shells and were covered in scorch marks. They were packed in ice to keep them cool. The man cut off the top of a nut, placed a straw in the small hole and handed it to me. In all my experience of drinking young coconuts in Asia and the Pacific islands, I have never tasted coconut juice so sweet. The roasting concentrates the sugar and makes it especially delicious. After drinking the juice, vendors cut the nut open so the jelly-like flesh can be spooned out and eaten.

Another thing I like in the markets of Asia is fresh sugar cane juice. The pure sugar cane taste is lovely and if it's poured over crushed ice, it's very refreshing, and not overpoweringly sweet. You can find sugar cane juice all through Asia and now, in Sydney, in Asian food centres, they press sugar cane through rollers and serve it up. But you have to tell them not to put lime or lemon into the juice. They think Australians want a more interesting flavour but it's the pure sugary juice that's so lovely. I first tasted it in Burma when I was quite young. I went to visit my grandmother who lived there then. That was before World War II but I still remember the way it tasted. Whenever we went out for a walk in the evening, we would stop and get some.

Things became so bad in Burma during and after the war that my grandmother's family had to walk out. They walked for a month to get to India. My husband, Reuben, was also born in Burma. When Burma was invaded by the Japanese, he and his brothers walked out. He was a teenager so he managed the journey slightly better than my grandmother. She was fifty at the time and it was a very bad experience.

When I was a child in Sri Lanka, my father would take me with him to the markets. He used to love going, but I hated the crowds, the noise, the smells. I'd just sit in the car and pretend it wasn't happening. The municipal markets in Colombo are huge and although they're covered by a roof, the sides are open, due to the stifling tropical heat. There's nothing to keep the flies out. Flyscreens? Forget it! Never heard of them! So the meat just hangs in the stalls and flies swarm all around.

Let me tell you, it was not a pretty sight. No wonder I loathed those excursions. Needless to say, any meat purchased was very well washed and very thoroughly cooked. Remembering my distaste for the markets, it seems ironic that now, when I travel, the first place I head for is a local market because it is there one sees the food of the country at its freshest and best.

The most recent market I have visited was at Kuantan in Malaysia and it was very nice and clean. They had one section for fish, another for meat, and yet another for spices, so everyone goes to three or four sections. I particularly like the vegetables and fruit. In fact, left to myself, I would probably be a vegetarian.

Fish markets are always fascinating because in each country you get a different selection of fish, depending on which sea laps its shores. In Apia, Western Samoa, I really wanted to try the local food so I was taken to a market. There were big heaps of fish being landed; they were still flapping around, they were so fresh. There were reef fish and warm tropical fish and a kind of bony fish which was being fried and served on the spot.

In India, which has a collective sweet tooth, there are particular shops devoted to making particular sweets. I went to one place in Srinagar in Kashmir and saw *halvais* [confectioners] making *moti choor laddoo*, which translates as 'balls of pearls'. They drop a batter—made from pea flour and water, flavoured and coloured with pure saffron—through a perforated spoon into a huge brass pan of bubbling ghee. The batter forms tiny round balls, poetically referred to as pearls, which they scoop out of the hot ghee and soak in a syrup. When cool enough to handle, these are moulded into shapes the size of golf balls. They are very rich and delicious.

I've been to a sweet shop in Bombay where they have an enormous pair of beautiful brass scales and they weigh out anything you choose. I went mad and bought a big box full of sweets, as we were leaving that day and I didn't want to miss out. We tasted just a tiny bit of everything and then called the room boy in our hotel and asked if he would please take them away because they were just too much. He was delighted. You really have to be brought up on those sweets, they are so rich.

In Agra, famous for the Taj Mahal, there is a whole street devoted to making just one kind of sweet—preserved melon or *petha*. An enormous melon just like Chinese winter melon, dark green on the outside and with snow-white flesh within, is cut into large chunks and goes through various processes. The whole thing takes around three days. Those sweet makers are incredibly skilful—it's like a pane of glass by the time they finish, translucent in the middle with a thin coating of sugar all around. Once again you need a really sweet tooth because as it's crystallised, the taste is intensely sweet, but absolutely delicious. Yummy stuff.

At every Asian market there's freshly cooked food. The advantage of seeing it cooked in front of you is that you can judge which stall and which cook meet your standards of hygiene. It's not considered snack food, but rather an actual meal. You just sit and eat then and there, no tables or cloths, just a wooden table and stool.

And there's always beautiful, exotic fruit. I always carry a small fruit knife around with me so I can cut it myself if it's large. In the markets of Apia, I remember buying yellow-skinned passionfruit which is very sweet and juicy, but not as strongly perfumed as our Australian variety which might need some sugar to mellow its mouth-puckering sourness. There were also a few piles of mangosteens, which I immediately bought. The mangosteen is known as the 'Queen of Fruits' and within its hard purple shell are small, milky-white segments which are soft in texture and sweet-sour in flavour. The story is that the mangosteen is cooling to the system, and should always be eaten together with durian—the 'King of Fruits'—because durian is 'heaty' and has the reputation of being an aphrodisiac.

In Singapore, at one of the outdoor eating stalls, Reuben and I indulged ourselves and ate two whole durians, each followed by a dozen mangosteens. At the weekend markets in Bangkok, we were with some friends—real dinky-di Aussies—and I told them they'd have to excuse us because we were going to buy durian. I didn't think they'd appreciate the smell. But they tasted it and were mad about it. The average durian is about the size of a soccer ball and has a thick, dull green skin which looks, and is, spiky. At Asian markets they will open it for you but if opening it yourself, wear gardening gloves for protection. Inside, it has separate compartments, smooth and white, which hold pale-yellow custardy flesh clinging to large brown seeds. The best way to enjoy it is to pick up a seed in your fingers and suck off the soft custard. People fall about in shock and horror at the smell, and I must admit it's off-putting, especially from a distance, but once you taste it, you just notice a strong aroma, like a very ripe mango or a jackfruit—with perhaps a touch of garlic or strong cheese thrown in!

In the Thai markets, you see curry puffs being made. Some are tiny, sometimes just one bite size, and some are more substantial, but they all have beautiful detail. Every single one of them has a lovely rope edge which someone has very deftly done by hand. I've also seen paw paw salad being made. The stall-holders don't have graters, they just peel the paw paw and hold it in one hand and with a huge chopper they chop, chop, chop at it so the cuts are very close together, turn the fruit around and chop, chop, chop again. Then it slices off in layers of very fine julienne strips. Then they put all the wicked stuff into the mortar and pestle with the strips of paw paw: garlic, fish sauce, chillies and peanuts. It's made to order each time—just enough for each customer. Each vendor specialises in something and that's what they do all day, every day.

Produce differs according to latitude, too, of course. I remember a market in Delhi where there were beautiful guavas and, in Bangalore, which is situated on a cool plateau in Karnataka, I couldn't resist the flowers—such varied colours, and the smaller ones strung into necklaces, bracelets and hair ornaments, and all so cheap.

When I was quite little, we used to go for holidays up to Kandy, a hill station in Sri Lanka. My grand-uncle had a farm, or estate as they're called up there. They ran a couple of cows and grew luscious fruit. Whenever we went up there for a holiday, Dad would always stop at the market on the way. He was a market person: he wouldn't have dreamed of going to a grocery store, he wanted to get right where the action was. He'd buy tiny woven baskets full of palm sugar. It was solid but crumbly with a flavour similar to maple sugar. You can also buy it in larger shapes for chopping and cooking or in the form of honey.

The best time to go to the markets in Asia is in the early morning when it is coolest. As the day goes on, it gets hotter and hotter, and all you can think of is getting back to the air-conditioned hotel. When people talk about the humidity of Sydney, I tell them they don't know what humidity is. I remember getting off a plane at Jakarta Airport and as I was walking towards the terminal, I thought I must be in the slip-stream of a jet engine, it was like a sauna bath, as if I was getting hit by hot steam.

The other time to go marketing in Asia is in the evening. Everything comes to life when the day has cooled down. Night markets sell everything from clothes, paintings and handicrafts to all sorts of foodstuffs, but not vegetables because they're always purchased in the morning. They're bought fresh each day, taken home and cooked straight away. Since most homes don't have a refrigerator, food has to be bought and cooked and eaten quickly.

The Flemington markets in Sydney are great, too. They are full of characters and if you go week after week, you get to know who sells what. There was a man who used to sell basil, rhubarb and the most beautiful bunches of mint and I thought to myself, I bet he keeps chickens or cows or something because that mint was so lush, it was the best I have ever seen. The Flemington sellers are quite specialised: for example, people who sell Italian parsley and basil don't generally have coriander. You go to the Vietnamese stalls for the fresh South-East Asian herbs. Or the Chinese stalls for the fuzzy melons, chunks of winter melon and the straight, sometimes thorny, stems of Chinese boxthorn which is so highly regarded as a health food. There are bunches of what is loosely called 'Chinese spinach' but which is really amaranth, and of course, the many vegetables which are lumped together as 'Chinese cabbages' but which have their distinct textures and flavours.

Greeks and Italians sell nuts, cheese, pasta, dried beans and dried fruit. Islanders sell cassava and taro and yams. Egyptians and other Middle-Eastern people sell and buy *meloukhia*—large bunches of green leaves which are finely chopped to make a soup of the same name. It's like taking a trip to half-a-dozen countries in one morning.

I usually go [to Flemington] about 9.30 on a Saturday morning—if you go past 10.30, you miss the best choice. As I go down the aisle nearest the main doorway, as you face the markets in Shed D, on the left side, there's usually someone grating coconuts. There are two ways to buy it: with some of the brown skin grated in or, for about $2 extra a kilo, more finely and carefully grated. It's really good and I use it for making salads and sambals. The stall's run by Fijian Indians.

When you are brought up in the East, you know that stall-holders will ask for at least twice as much as they hope to get and you are supposed to bargain. It's meant to be enjoyable on both sides. But if it were me selling, I wouldn't dream of quoting a price twice what I expected to get. I would make it as reasonable as possible, make sure I was covered and say, 'Right, that's what it is.'

But Reuben is marvellous at haggling. It embarrasses me, especially when I go to Flemington. I think, good heavens, $4 for a tray of peaches, and they've tended those trees, and sprayed them, and picked the fruit and transported it. In season, most produce is cheap and we are so lucky in Australia. Reuben always ends up saying to me, 'Charmaine, whose side are you on?' 🙴

Heaven on a
satay stick

PRIA VISWALINGAM
TV presenter

"My father, a doctor, was born in Malaysia to Sri Lankan Tamil parents; my mother, also Tamil, was from Colombo—where they met and married. They lived in England while my father completed his studies, then returned to Malaysia where I was born, in Kota Bharu, on the east coast. When I was two, we settled in Kuala Lumpur and my father opened a practice in the Chinese area. Everyone said he was mad, but he took on the hardworking Chinese on their own terms and worked seven days a week, right up to the time we left the country. We lived in shacks in the early years, but they were nice shacks, old wooden houses built on stilts, gardens full of snakes, and the one I remember particularly fondly was on Gurney Road.

We were real bicycle freaks, we three brothers and other boys in the neighbourhood. We used to cycle in the early evenings and the suburbs were, and still are, a hive of activity, particularly towards dusk. The older boys would be out playing soccer and I recall these lovely images of a Chinese granddad or an amah with a child, freshly showered, in pyjamas, going for their evening walk prior to dinner, ambling past at a deathly pace, child in tow, as we hooned around, racing each other on our bicycles.

At one end of Gurney Road was a tiny rubber plantation, about a quarter of an acre with around twelve trees, and it was great for snakes. They used to slither across the road and we would ride over them on our bicycles. At the other end, there was a kampung or Malay-style village. You had to navigate your way down a narrow clay path, which was often muddy from frequent thunderstorms, up a slight hill, and there, at the top, was a classic kampung, chooks running around, seven little houses, all on stilts, with lovely brushed-sand front yards.

It could have been plucked from the middle of the Terengganu coastline, completely authentic, and they were simple village folk, really soft. They didn't have very much but they would offer us cordial and we'd play with the kampung kids, these snotty-nosed guys. We'd chase the chickens around or let the kids have our bicycles, and occasionally we'd take them to our house to play badminton. It was like having a bit of the country smack-bang next door, and we'd go to school the next day and be in history class, learning about kampung life and Malay culture and roots, and we could really relate to it because in the evening we could go home and experience it. It's a shame my children probably won't experience that level of cultural interplay or camaraderie. We lived a middle-class existence but we were able to mix with the kampung kids, though they were more wary of us than we were of them.

Family holidays were royal affairs, and most years we'd go to Singapore for Christmas. Mum would spend the morning with the servants, making sandwiches and drinks; we'd load up the car and then have to wait for Dad to turn up—he was always late. We would be starving because we were supposed to leave at four to miss the rush hour and we'd finally get out of the house at about seven, the three of us in the back seat, Mum and Dad in the front. We'd head off on the 240-mile drive to Singapore but the first stop was always Kajang, an hour from KL. Kajang had, and apparently still has, the best satay in Malaysia.

We would lose the city lights pretty quickly, drive through rubber estates, and then over this particular crest and on the horizon we could see a neon glow. Kajang! Our stomach juices would start flowing, we could practically smell the satay in the air. Finally we would pull up and run inside, and we used to eat forty satay sticks each—they were a little smaller than those you see in Australia, but it was a matter of honour, you had to eat forty each. The hawkers would count up the sticks, that's how they charged. Then we'd collapse back in the car and Dad would drive the rest of the night to Singapore. We'd arrive around two in the morning and be carried, bleary-eyed, into Aunty Pari's house and put to bed. The next morning we'd wake to the sound of traffic on Clemenceau Avenue, just off Orchard Road.

Singapore had a particular sound and a particular feel, it was exciting, a big, snappy city. The first thing we used to do was go to C.K. Tang's department store which had the toy section from heaven. We'd walk in, eyes hanging out of our heads, and we were only allowed to buy one toy, but we'd spend a whole morning there.

We had cousins to play with, which was always great fun, lots of Enid Blyton-style adventures. I remember an uncle of ours, Uncle Chong Beng, an urbane Chinese gentleman—everyone was called uncle or aunty as a sign of respect—who used to take us up to World War II Japanese dugouts, places the Japanese kept prisoners, or he would uncover an old cavern and tell us it was where the Japanese used to hide. He would regale us with these wondrous—and sometimes suspect—stories and we'd sit, listening in awe, with eyes like saucers. It was all quite spooky.

Singapore represented activity: it was denser, closer, clean streets, even back then. In contrast, in those days, KL was sleepier: it was quiet, pretty. In Singapore, people were busy, it was a happening place, the shops were more interesting than those in KL and always had the latest of everything: toys, running shoes, model aeroplanes—which we were all fanatical about, we were Airfix freaks. We'd bring our catalogues and buy the latest releases or the paint we'd read about in our *Beano* and *Dandy* comics or English football magazines.

One of my favourite memories of Singapore is going to sleep in the afternoon, after lunch. There was a certain cicada with a particularly high-pitched song and it was so soothing, lying there, fan going quietly, windows and door open, listening to the cicadas in the dense trees. I used to drift off into this deep, deep sleep.

In Malaysia, we always travelled in groups with other families, friends, cousins and so on, we never really had solitary family holidays. The hilltop resort of Fraser's Hill was another favourite spot, always filled with more languid adventures. It was built by the Poms, thirty kilometres off the beaten track from Kuala Kubu Bharu, about an hour north-east of KL. You wind your way up to a point they call the Gap and the traffic becomes one-way—odd hours one direction, even hours the other. From there it was seven kilometres to the resort with a dozen two-storey colonial bungalows. It was like a little piece of England in the middle of Malaysia. And every morning these thick mists rolled in over the mountains; it had a lovely cool climate, around 17 or 18 degrees.

I always remember the Chinese housekeeper there and his wife in starched white collars, and everything served in silver, with solid silver cutlery. The toast would come out sliced and in those little toast holders, perfectly brown. At night they'd light the fires. And crisp white sheets. Mum would tuck us in so tightly we could hardly breathe.

After breakfast we had the whole day to fill with assorted cousins, brothers and friends, and we used to walk in the cool, lush greenery, ferns resplendent, rhinoceros beetles, huge millipedes ambling past, large fruit and luxuriant flowers—roses the size of your hand. We'd go for jungle treks or swim in crystal-clear streams which sprang up all over the place after overnight rain.

During Singapore holidays there was always something to do, somewhere to go, but during the day at Fraser's Hill we'd spend a lot of time together, not doing very much, just walking and listening to the older boys talking about *Mad* comics and girls. We younger boys didn't understand and we'd giggle and poke each other in the back and then we'd get clouted by one of the older boys who'd yell, '*Shut* up.'

We had to be creative, which is probably why it was memorable. And it was absolutely silent after bustling, heaving Singapore. The bungalows are still there, now somewhat lost among flashy new resorts. They are a bit shoddy nowadays, and unkempt, which, in a way, makes them somewhat sad and forlorn.

The other trips were north to Ipoh or Penang, and most times we'd leave on the weekend, the car packed to the hilt and everyone throwing up on the way because we were dreadful travellers. My father would be furious and yell, 'Why don't you just *tell* me you're going to throw up and I'll stop the car!' He used to buy these lovely old cars with leather upholstery and we used to barf all over them. Night trips were fine because we slept, but on the day trips we would stare out of the window, thoroughly bored, watching nothing much go past. The roads weren't that good in those days, twisting and turning, full of ghastly lorries belching black smoke, and by the time you realised and opened a window, it was too late. He'd get out and stomp up and down while Mum cleaned up the mess and then we'd find a rest house.

Rest houses, a great colonial legacy, can still be seen. We would pull off the road at one of these grand old colonial bungalows with marvellous high ceilings, big ceiling fans, cane furniture, lovely big bathrooms. We'd clean up and then we'd sit down and have cucumber and tuna sandwiches, on fine white bread, a cup of tea or the obligatory orange juice, and we'd pass an hour and a half there, not doing much, cooling off under the fans, and then back in the car.

My father's friend had a company bungalow in Penang, right on the beach at Batu Ferringhi, where all the big hotels are now, but in those days it was just bungalows. We'd arrive at night, half asleep as usual, and the next morning we awoke to the salty smell of the sea. Memories of sharing beds with cousins, maybe four in one big bed, playing on the beach, going for swims in the ocean. Eating ourselves into a collective stupor. Early one morning, my father woke us. It was a beautiful grey dawn and this long fishing boat had just pulled up. The fisherman jumped out, announcing that he had fresh Tinggiri fish, which I think is Spanish mackerel. We bought it, took it indoors, and the ladies chopped it up and cooked this chilli-spicy, fried fish dish with rice.

Food was, and still is, a very important part of my life. My Dad was a real foodie, he introduced us to all tastes. He had a mate who went wild-boar hunting in Pahang Jungle, and around the same time each year, this chap would turn up, virtually under the cover of darkness, press the buzzer on the front door and whisper, 'Is your father in?' and he'd hand over a package and disappear. It would be a fresh-cut piece of wild boar, wrapped in banana leaf and paper. Next day, it was marinated and we'd have it that evening, curried, very hot, with stringhoppers—stringy noodles which look like nests, made from rice flour and steamed. We'd each have three or four, covered in *sothi*, a yellow, tangy coconut gravy, and eat it with the wild boar curry. It was the best curry in the world, even to this day.

Everywhere you go in Malaysia, at all times of day, there's food passing by, even in the deepest part of the suburbs. There was a range of hawkers who used to come by the house, around 5.30 in the evening. I was becoming a fat kid then and any time I'd see loose change lying around I'd whip it and save it for the hawkers. You'd hear a horn going *beep beep*, and it was the Chinese guy with *char sui bao* and *sui mais*. I'd run to the top of the road as soon as I heard him, buy a little collection and eat it by myself. I even got to the point where I'd stash it outside the house, under a bush, go and have dinner and later go out and eat it by myself. And dinner was always a serious affair, four or five different curries. We ate curry every day with our fingers. I still eat that way at home.

Then there was the *kush* man. It was sad, because this poor old man was bent over from carrying a long bamboo pole, two big tiffin carriers either side, all his life. They contained *kueh*, Malay cakes, and he walked from suburb to suburb, house to house, every day, for hours, selling these snacks. We would call him in and you could see him heave the weight off his shoulders and then give the tiniest little stretch before he had to pick it up and show us what he had.

Every other day, the bread man would come on his little motor bike, *toot toot* as he went, metal container perched on the back seat, overladen with all manner of breads and buns and sweet things draped off the back. Or the stringhopper man would come by, on a bicycle, with a metal container strapped to the back. He'd open the container, which was lined with banana leaves, and there was this wonderful aroma of freshly steamed stringhoppers which he served with a dollop of *gula melaka*, brown sugar.

Once every six months or so, the curry powder men would turn up in a Volkswagen van. There were two of them in the front and they'd get out, open the side door and there'd be a guy stuck inside, in the slight glow from the interior light, surrounded by curry and chilli powders in little clear packets. The smell was incredible and I don't know how this guy survived! When you walk past spice shops you still get that pungent odour of freshly-ground spices, but this van had it all. 'What would you like?' he'd say as he brought out freshly ground curry powder, chilli, coriander. They came from Palaniappa Mills and it was *the* place to go for spices. You could practically see the fumes emanating from the van as it went down the street, people falling off their bicycles and cars crashing in its wake.

There were these entrepreneur types who had little utes with a canopy on top, and they'd head to the market at 4 am, buy a stack of fish and vegetables, and drive to the suburbs where they'd sell it. The housewives or servants, if they didn't want to go shopping, would wait for the man to turn up. He always had a splendid variety of fish, kept on blocks of ice and covered with gunnysacks, and we'd pick what we wanted. I used to sit there salivating! We always bought three or four fish just for the dogs—ours used to love the stuff. Mum would come out half lost in a book, the servants would come out and we'd come out, and we'd all poke and prod and be told this is this fish, this is that fish. He'd tot up what we bought and we paid at the end of the month. We brats would try to nick a fish when he wasn't looking, but he knew because he had a fixed smile which would contort into a scowl as soon as Mother left.

There were religious festivals four times a year, and they were non-stop eating affairs, especially Hari Raya, the Malay and Ramadan celebration. Each race would visit the other during festivals, so Malay, Chinese and Indian friends would visit Westerners at Christmas; Malays, Chinese and Westerners would visit Tamils during Deepavali, and so on. Everyone would have open house, so masses of food had to be prepared.

Take Hari Raya, for example. We started in the morning and Dad used to warn us, '*Don't* eat everything at the first house, we have twelve to go to.' Of course we never listened and there'd be piles of home-cooked *rendang* sitting there, which the ladies had spent all week cooking. We'd stuff ourselves, get to the next house, manage a few morsels, and then we'd be dead—and we had ten more houses to go. Dad would berate us, as we sat burping in the back of the car or slothing around from house to house, moaning 'Can we go now?'

Chinese New Year was great, as we all used to get *hong pao* or envelopes with lucky money inside them. Deepavali meant curries all round, and we used to have a party, usually Christmas, which was the only thing we celebrated because we weren't overly religious and we didn't observe anything Tamil, except of course when it suited Father.

I've lived in the West longer than I've lived in the East, but I have many fond memories of those times. I was only twelve when we left, but I had a range of cultural experiences at my fingertips and it was a very rich life. To be able to speak other languages, and mix with Chinese, Indians, Malays, in what was a very warm, sincere place. It's nice to know I have roots elsewhere, that I come from a country like Malaysia where there are age-old traditions and a respect for elders.

In Australia, I am different and people will always ask, 'Where are you from?' In Malaysia, I'm just part of the crowd. I am Asian, I do Asian things, I behave in an Asian way when I'm there. It was a very tactile place, guys used to put their arms around each other; there was a lot of spontaneous warmth between people, without the reservation inherent in Western societies. I treasure my memories of a languid life, of gentle people, of great food. All that will remain with me forever. **99**

Chapter 6

THE GLOBAL VILLAGE

World travellers
and adventurers

On top of
the world

SORREL WILBY
Adventurer

"An adventurer? I like to think of myself as a culture vulture. Even when I was a kid, I was really inspired by *National Geographic*. It presented a world so far beyond my comprehension—a whole gamut of people, costumes, music, sound, light and extremes of colour. I felt my pulse quicken every time I picked up one of those magazines; a rush of excitement about what was *out there* beyond the familiar bricks and mortar of Sydney.

With the classic logic of a twelve-year-old, I decided that the only way you could get to all those people, cultures and landscapes was by becoming a photographer with *National Geographic*. So that was what I set my sights on.

The first time I fell in love with the world was on an eight-month four-wheel-drive trip around Australia. I followed that with my first overseas trip, cycling 17,000 kilometres through Asia over 18 months. It was a novel experience—I'd never even ridden a bike before. I learned to climb on that trip, following it up with a 3000 kilometre solo trek across Tibet, a 6500 kilometre traverse of the Himalaya and an expedition in which my husband, Chris Ciantar, and I scaled all the highest peaks on the African continent. If you say all that very quickly, it sounds like a doddle!

Because of my expeditions and books, people assume I'm completely besotted with mountains. And, yes, I am, but as a backdrop or a platform on which I can sit, quite literally, and look out and regain an insight into the big picture. If I've just visited a mountain village, I can climb higher and look down on it, and all the small pieces of what I've learnt can be fitted together. I don't know of any other way of travelling which gives you this perspective.

I've been born into a generation in which mountains are really the only places where you can still find people who haven't had their tribalism—or what makes them culturally unique—stripped away. In remote mountain regions, people live closer to what I consider to be the truth.

One of the most fascinating places I have been is Arunachal Pradesh, in India, where the mountains of Tibet come down like fingers from knuckles with the valleys in between. All those valleys are smothered with impenetrable jungle so you have a hundred and fifty different tribal groups, each one living on its own ridge top, and although you can see the next village, to get to it is a nightmare. And, when you do, the people speak another language, have an entirely different set of spiritual beliefs and customs and yet, as the crow flies, they are only five or ten kilometres away. I find that amazing. The scenery is just a bonus. It's the social anthropology, the little details you catch out of the corner of your eye that really fascinate me.

Each place I visit, I find a tiny place for it in my heart, always for different reasons. But a very special place to me— not somewhere that I could ever live, but where I've left behind a little bit of myself—is Arkwasiye, in Ethiopia, at the crossroads of many routes which go through the Simien Mountains. The landscape is so biblical, it's like stepping back two thousand years. Chris and I arrived after a long and very hot day on the trail, pitched our tents, and when we woke next morning, our camp was surrounded by inquisitive children who had never seen white people before. They were so natural and unaffected; they stroked the back of my hand and planted little kisses on my knuckles, rested their heads against my knees and took turns at climbing into my lap for a cuddle.

I couldn't leave the kids alone, nor they me, so we all wandered down into the thick of the Saturday market. Within seconds of entering the open-market mêlée, I was completely swamped. Toothless old people were grabbing onto me, cupping my face in their hands and kissing both my cheeks. Men were reaching out to shake my hand and the kids accompanying me looked as if they'd just won some fabulous trophy in a footie match. I was buoyed by the crowd, carried by their waves of curiosity and affection. I don't think a place or a group of people has touched me more. Their trust and unconditional acceptance made a gift I will cherish forever.

In that tiny, otherwise insignificant village, I came to realise why this whole sad and sorry continent endured. While we in the West despair for Africa and look at it only in terms of its overwhelming past failings, Africa itself chooses to rejoice in its unknowable future.

Two-and-a-half years later, we went back to Arkwasiye as I wanted to film there. I was afraid everything would be changed, that it would now be on a tourist route. The first time we left, the head of the village presented us with a chicken and I'd felt empty-handed, with nothing to give in return. We walked in, for the second time, and the kids just ran up with the same welcome—all that had changed was they were two-and-a-half years older. They were devastated when we left the second time and we all cried and cried. If I died tomorrow, it would be with the biggest smile on my face, knowing that I had had a truly priceless experience.

Would I return there? I don't normally go back over ground I have trodden. I'm very much a Gemini in that respect. There is so much more to explore and I'm always conscious there is limited time. I could go on for ever learning in a place like Arkwasiye but I wouldn't be challenged. In terms of second homes, I would choose Kathmandu. The first time I went there was in 1985, in order to get into Tibet via Lhasa by road. I'd done my climbing training in India and it made sense to go to Kathmandu rather than back to Hong Kong to get a visa for Tibet. I'd imagined Kathmandu would just be an incidental stopover, a base camp.

I found this big city full of travellers. And cafés and bakeries—so different from India. But despite all those Westerners congregating there, Kathmandu is medieval. I remember at first light one morning, about five—I always get up early, it's the best part of the day—everything was still as still, I went for a walk along all these cobbled alleys. I went into one back alley which opened to another and then another and I felt myself disappearing into the most intricate maze. I ended up in this little courtyard which opened out into another tiny square and there was a really heavy mist hanging over everything, right down to street level, and it was like walking through fog, time travelling, just the crispest of sounds cutting through, like the occasional bark of a dog. There was a deadened quality about it, like when it snows. What always appeals to me about snow falling is that it's the sound of absolute peace.

All of a sudden, the King of Nepal's horses—the most immaculate beasts, with coats groomed to a metallic sheen—galloped past. I felt them brush past me, otherwise I would have thought it was a dream. I turned the next corner and there was an old woman, with smallpox scars all over her face, and she was laying marigolds on a little altar at the entrance to a temple and all these little fragments of gold stood out against the fog.

There's an energy in Kathmandu. It's a city of crossroads which don't rub and create friction, but create electricity. It's a totally different place at seven in the evening than it is at five in the morning—and at any time, you can pick any street and have an altogether different experience to what is happening just around the corner.

Things happened to me in Kathmandu like a chain reaction. I'd meet one person, who'd introduce me to another, and so it went on—and it still does, every time I return. I ended up waiting weeks for my Tibetan visa and in the end, I decided to enter illegally. I hid in the back of a truck, under a tarp, for four days, until we got to Lhasa and then I collapsed.

My friends in Kathmandu thought I was mad and when I got back, they said they thought I'd never be seen again. Then I remembered they'd all said these emotional goodbyes, as if I were going off to war. It's fortunate to be so naive, sometimes. If I'd known what I know now, I wouldn't have set out on at least three-quarters of my adventures! Like walking across Tibet, for example. I was so unprepared—physically, mentally and emotionally. I decided to walk because that rugged landscape is not for cycling—too many flat tyres. At one stage, I stayed with a nomad's family for a few days. They adopted me and it was the weirdest sensation to be sharing their tent and food and not being able to communicate. Whenever I smell juniper burning, I think of that interlude and I almost burst into tears, not because it was so difficult, but because it was a defining moment, a time when I was forced to think about who I am, and feeling humbled by the sheer beauty of simply being accepted for that.

We need adventures—to either have them ourselves, if we

can, or learn about them—because they fulfil our dreams. My adventures have been small by some people's standards, but against all odds I've overcome difficulties and that's had a far-reaching effect on other people's lives. I've had letters from people about to undergo brain surgery, and they have read one of my books and from what I've written they've gained courage. It's not about people following in your foot-steps, in the most literal of senses, but it's about the human spirit.

What adventurers do is to inspire people to achieve in their own way. I enjoy being an adventurer, not because people put me on a pedestal but because they can look at me and say, 'Well, there's a Joe Average girl but she's gone off and done all that. I wonder what I can do now?' Being a woman, and doing what I do, is very important because half the human race just can't cancel me out!

The places closest to my heart are those where I've had realisations. Not great visions—just crystal-clear moments of understanding of what the world is and what it represents. **"**

Touching the face
of the universe

GLENN A. BAKER
Rock historian and writer

"Travel should not be easy. The world is sharp, abrasive, at times intimidating, exhilarating and rewarding, and you've got to tread carefully. I travel with a different agenda, with a different perspective. I'm drawn instinctively to the odd, the curious, the unexpected.

For me, it's not about encountering mountains and buildings and bus timetables, it's to do with unexpected situations or people who are as opposed to me, in the way they live, think and act, as they can possibly be. It is very important to me to be able to go out and touch the face of the world. I'm also drawn to countries that are undergoing great change— all the certainties are no longer there, there is a sense of confusion. To places with history, where some human drama has unfolded, and to places with a very different culture. It is the experiences rather than the country itself which remain in my heart.

For example, I was in East Berlin in early 1990, I'd gone through Checkpoint Charlie and, even though the Wall had begun to come down, it was still very much two Germanys and a protected communist state. Honnecker had gone, the party was in disgrace and everyone knew it was all about to come crumbling down.

I was walking down a side street in East Berlin and I saw a cherry picker, up against the side of a building, with a man on it. I looked really closely and saw that the building was the headquarters of the East German Communist Party and the logo was being removed from the wall. It was so symbolic, this was the end of communism in East Germany, and I was the only person in the whole world, standing there, watching it being dismantled.

One of the funniest things—well, funny in retrospect—that happened to me was at the same time. Parts of the wall remained, but very menacing East German border guards were still hanging around and looking rather trigger happy. I was there with my hammer and chisel, to souvenir a piece of the wall, and I noticed a group of East German youths on top of the wall—a very brave thing to do. They had a boom box and they were dancing, celebrating their new-found freedom. They saw me and decided I could be a party animal—I looked pretty feral, like a rugged, good-time Westerner. They said, 'Come up, come up', and they put their arms down and pulled me on to the wall.

I was getting into it, boogeying on down and shaking my booty, having a great time, when all of a sudden, in the euphoria of the moment, I noticed something was missing. It was the music. It was them. They'd gone, in a puff of smoke, and I was left on top of the wall on my own. Then I realised why. I looked down and there was a squad of four East German soldiers and they were making unmistakable signs, meaning *get down*. I complied immediately. So there was this overweight, bearded Westerner, tearing his hands and feet, trying to climb down the Berlin Wall—and on the Eastern side, there were a couple of hundred Czech schoolgirls, on an excursion, *pissing* themselves laughing.

I got to Vietnam in early 1990, a matter of months after they changed the regulations and made it easier for tourists. Hanoi was completely untouched, there were virtually no automobiles, people rode bicycles along empty streets lined with tamarind trees. It was a city of lakes and there were colonial buildings painted in muted shades of yellow. It was a place frozen in time, as though preserved in aspic, and it struck me that it was not just untouched from the days of the Vietnam War, it was unchanged from the days of the French. Nothing had altered in this place since the 1950s. From the moment I arrived, I felt as if I were the only outsider in this legendary, almost mythical city. But within a year, there were cranes on the skyline, cars, trucks and buses belching fumes, motor bikes and smog.

All I had seen before then was the Asia that aped the West, that wanted to be London, New York, Paris. We all despair over the encroachment of civilisation and the fact that every place in the world is beginning to look like everywhere else, everyone wears the same patterned T-shirts, plays the same CDs, wears the same wristwatches and baseball caps. Nowadays, all you see is a slight variation on the world you know. But Vietnam in early 1990 was pure Asia.

The other aspect of travel I enjoy is finding the odd and curious, and coming across it unexpectedly. I was in Japan in the castle city of Kanazawa, known for its cherry blossoms, its imperial architecture and for a sedate, traditional way of life. I was reading a guidebook and noted that on May 22, the Haemorrhoid Curing Buddha would be on display at the San-boji Temple. Now, I'm one of those people long accustomed to the fact that whatever may be on in a place is going to be a week before or after I am there. As I once wrote, 'The Nude Teenage Drum Majorette Memorial March Past has always eluded me.' So I couldn't believe my luck—I was in Kanazawa at the right time.

I jumped in a cab, arrived at this ramshackle old wooden building, made my way past a queue of fidgeting petitioners into the temple and looked up to see him—a standing Buddha, I should point out—nestled there in the rafters. I didn't exactly require the services of said Buddha but I can't tell you how *delighted* I was to know there *was* one. It makes me sleep better at night. I like the idea of a world that *has* a Haemorrhoid Curing Buddha. I'm glad to know that there are arcane practices and curious phenomena occurring in the world and that, if I try hard enough, I can find them.

I travelled to the island of Sulawesi in Indonesia and had a bone-shattering, rattling, nine-hour ride from the capital of Ujong Pandeng to the cosmic realms of Torajaland. It is actually one of the most visited places in Indonesia but more by Europeans than Australians, who tend to go to Bali.

The people of Torajaland are largely animists and they have an ancient funeral ritual which involves burying people after a very long mourning period. They are buried inside the cliffs in little chambers hewn from the rock and the deceased are represented on balconies outside the *liangs*—mountainside graves—by puppets, almost like mannequins. In fact, they are the objects of art thieves the world over.

Torajans have a theory that when you die, you are not actually dead until you have a funeral, which is the central part of their life. Officially, until the funeral, the person is really only sick, so the body is put in a room, some very basic frontier-style embalming is applied, and it's brought three meals a day. Now, if it is a *really* important person and mourners have to come from all over the country, or even the world, the funeral can take up to two years to organise. When the body is finally buried, the Torajans slaughter buffaloes and pigs— or, in the case of an important person, a couple of hundred buffaloes, which may include a precious white buffalo, and a thousand pigs—and the body is finally put to rest.

All the time they are going about these bizarre funeral

rituals, the Torajans are pretty much out of it. They wear a long bamboo tube slung over their shoulders, full of very potent palm wine, around 100 per cent proof, with a little tube leading from the tube to their mouth, and they are permanently plastered! These people live for death. They spend their lives, some of them in a state of near permanent intoxication, planning the next funeral. Why would you want to go and lie on a beach and read a Stephen King novel when you can experience something like that?

More than ten years ago, I travelled to Borneo and sailed up the Mahakam River on a barge. It was pure jungle, monkeys swinging from the trees, villagers cheerfully performing their ablutions and doing their laundry by the riverside, and after a couple of days we arrived at a Dayak village. We were formally received and there was a ceremony where we were inducted into this Stone Age tribe. We dressed in leaves, painted our faces white and danced with the witch doctor. We slept in the *lamin*, the long house, and I was absorbed totally into this ancient and seemingly untouched world. It was all I'd ever imagined the real Borneo would be.

On the last day, I wanted to say goodbye to the chief and give him my best wishes. He was an imposing figure, although not as agile as the witch doctor, who danced so ferociously he would have struck terror into Michael Jackson's heart. I asked directions and someone pointed to a hut on the rise. As I walked towards it, I noticed a long, slender aerial poking out of the chief's hut and presumed it must be for emergencies, some sort of short wave radio. I knocked on the door—as much as you can knock on thatch—and the chief's wife came out. I told her I wanted to say goodbye to the chief and she replied, 'Can you come back later? He's watching *Dynasty* right now.'

Hamburg has a great attraction for me, not for the Reeperbahn but the Kaiserkellar where the Beatles played. Hamburg features strongly in Beatles history and there are many landmarks that any child of the sixties just has to see. The attraction isn't just musical though. Someone had told me about an old sea captain called Harry. He had come back from the sea and opened a shop on Bernhardt Knoch Strasse, the same street that houses Hamburg's Sex Museum, which, of course, is at number 69. Harry's Harbour Bazaar is the most extraordinary emporium of ephemera I have ever laid eyes on. Harry opened a coin shop and then got his old seafaring mates to bring him back artefacts from various parts of the world: fertility dolls, carvings, stuffed beasts, talismans, and he started to buy out the shops next door and underneath him. He ended up with 22 rooms and in those 22 rooms are the treasures of Africa, the Orient, the mysterious East. A veritable Pandora's Box. I've told many people about it but nobody seems as interested as I am. And so it dawned on me that what brings me joy does not necessarily bring joy to others.

When I returned from a visit to South Korea in 1993, there was only one story I wanted to write—about the most visited place in the country, with more than 100,000 tourists a year. South Korea has temples, pagodas, factories and gardens but it also has the Cold War's last stand-off—the last great, heavily defended and fortified border in the world. A million troops on full alert. Men sitting in trucks with engines running, gripping the steering wheel, waiting. We signed waivers saying that the Americans and the South

Korean Army took no responsibility for our heads being blown off and we were put on a bus, told not to make any sudden movements towards the other side, and taken to a hut right on the border where North Korean soldiers made menacing gestures and pressed their faces against the window, leering at us. This wasn't a tour, this was the real thing. These two countries are mortal enemies, annihilation is on their minds and there had been a great deal of bloodshed in that area, many people had been killed there.

I was in Beirut in 1996 and it was in a state of crumbling disrepair, they had torn down 350 buildings and were about to tear down another 350. One that was still intact, on the waterfront by the Corniche, had this giant sign painted on its side saying: 'Hard Rock Café Beirut: Opening Soon'. Underneath it were three military tanks, covered in sheets of clear plastic, and next to them stood a soldier wearing a beret, his rifle dangling idly by his side. We asked his permission and, with a slight shrug, he allowed us to take a photo. A few weeks later I was at home watching the news on television, a story about the Israelis bombing Beirut for the first time in 14 years, and I recognised the Hard Rock Café sign. What I had thought was a great photo opportunity turned out to be the front line of Beirut defence!

So many components of travel are, by necessity, duplicated. You must check in, carry your bags, wait in departure lounges. It doesn't matter where you go, there are certain things you *have* to do. Once that's over, you don't then want to duplicate your holiday experience, the idea is to try and make it as astonishing as you possibly can. It doesn't always have to be bizarre. In fact, the most precious place in the world, my most indelible experience—the one that I rank number one—was not all that bizarre.

I was in Antarctica with my wife, Lorelle, and we'd sailed from Tierra Del Fuego on a boat called the *Akademik Sergei Vavilov*. We'd sailed past extraordinary icebergs, visited penguin rookeries and elephant seal colonies, and it was an astounding experience. Then one day we arrived in a place called Paradise Bay. It was a Sunday morning, I recall, and we got into rubber Zodiac boats and travelled around the Bay. Surrounding us was this glacial wall, a hundred feet high, with blue-tinged ice, pockmarked, like cathedral windows. And the ice was in a state of constant, wrenching change. It screamed. We were told that it was not uncommon for tonnes of it to break off and go crashing into the water.

There was no other noise beyond the screeching of the glacier ice and we watched as an iceberg slid by with maybe fifteen crab-eating seals lying on it, basking in the sun. Under the boat we could occasionally see penguins, travelling at around forty kilometres an hour, like little darts, going ping, ping, through the water. And then, just as we thought this was absolutely glorious, three huge humpback whales started playing tag around the boat, around and around, going under, going down, flapping their tails, spurting water in the air, playing with us, playing *for* us, but playing so delicately and so carefully that we were never in any danger. I remember sitting in the Zodiac thinking that if I had to surrender my passport tomorrow, if I could never travel again, it would be okay, I'd seen this, the last pristine continent, the perfect world, the way it was a long time before man.

I was on a panel at a book fair once with George Negus and someone asked us what were the worst places we'd been to.

We both tried to give the same answer simultaneously—that if you really like travelling, if you take great joy in it, there are no 'worst places'. I travel with an open mind and a sense of humour which opens most doors. If you are prepared to go out and face the world with a smile on your face and not judge it, and certainly not judge it by your standards, it's surprising how much people will give you, how much they will open their lives, their minds and their hearts to you. What you take to a place is essentially what you are going to bring away from it. **))**

Mountain
highs

TIM MACARTNEY-SNAPE
Mountaineer

"From early in my life, I was imprinted with the notion that the most exciting places you could go to were mountains. This has been continually reinforced by experience. I grew up on a farm in what was then the highlands of Tanganyika [now Tanzania] at an altitude of about 6000 feet. Our farm was called Irundi after a hill on the southern boundary of the property. Irundi Hill wasn't very big but I'll always remember the first time I was taken up there by my parents. We went for a picnic one Sunday on the saddle of the ridge and I was excited by the hill itself because in the gullies there grew all sorts of interesting vegetation. I'd heard my father talking of hyenas and leopards which used to take shelter in those thickets, so it was certainly more interesting than the grazing country of our farm. From then on, I thought of mountains as being places which had something extra to offer.

When I was eight, I was sent to boarding school as there were no schools in our area. It was a two-day drive from home along a dirt track through fascinating country. School was in the north of Tanzania, at Arusha, situated on the slopes of a 15,000-ft volcano called Mount Meru. I was there for four years and most days we looked out of the windows of the classrooms and we could see this big volcano rising in the distance. Sometimes during the cool dry season it would be sprinkled with snow on top.

Eighty kilometres to the east was Kilimanjaro which, again, you could see on clear days and, of course, as a young boy, I wanted more than anything to climb those peaks. Unfortunately we left Africa before I was considered old enough—it would have been a serious undertaking for a boy of twelve because of the altitude and the wildlife. You would have to have taken an armed guard in those days. So that was a great disappointment and I suppose not having that urge fulfilled made me desire mountain climbing even more.

My family moved to Australia and, luckily, I was sent to a place called Timbertop in Victoria. When I was fifteen, my schoolmates and I had permission to explore the Victorian Alps around Mount Buller every weekend. Come Friday afternoon, we would get our packs ready, having submitted a hiking plan which was modified if it was too adventurous or too outrageous. If everything was okay, we'd head out the school gate until Sunday evening when we were expected back. Climbing hills is a great teacher. Being young and wanting to prove myself, I typically loaded up with as much gear as I could carry. I discovered that was a dumb thing for an unfit boy to do. I had a sore back, aching legs and lungs and wanted to give up there and then. But you have to persevere if you've got to get to camp. You can't turn back, so you discover you have much more strength than you gave yourself credit for when things first got tough.

You learn to manage adversity, to cope with difficult tasks by breaking them down to more manageable chunks. You learn to look after yourself. When I finally took up mountaineering—that is, technical climbing—at university, my parents urged me to be careful and not do anything stupid. It must have been quite a difficult thing for them to come to terms with, but they never discouraged me.

My theory is that people have always found mountains to be attractive. From a geographic perspective, mountains have a profound impact on the country surrounding them. They attract water and are the source of most rivers and often the fertile plains below. Mountain weather is fascinating—it's wild and unpredictable. Indeed, it's the weather that I fear most in the mountains; it's the factor which causes most accidents and has nearly caused my demise on several occasions. One of the most memorable was on Mount Sarmiento in Tierra del Fuego. We were climbing a lower slope which was composed of glass-hard ice and were unroped so we could move faster on the moderately angled slope. The weather did not seem threatening but suddenly a wind of hurricane strength slammed into us and we found ourselves fighting for our lives. One of us was picked up and thrown onto the ice. Below him were giant crevasses and cliffs but he managed to arrest his fall by thrusting his arm into a crack in the ice.

Unfortunately, the force wrenched his shoulder out of its socket. We could do nothing to reduce the dislocation; it took two long days to get him down to his yacht—our only means of travel back to civilisation and medical help on the other side of the Straits of Magellan. Our team split in two, and three of us remained to climb the mountain in better conditions. It turned out to be a stunningly beautiful climb.

Once you get above the snow line, it's almost like stepping out of the world as we know it into another sort altogether. Because of its newness in your range of experiences, this environment of glaciers and snow is very exciting. The view you get, the lofty situation you're in, that top-of-the-world feeling is exhilarating. You can see a photo of a mountain and say it's really beautiful, an incredible scene, breathtaking, but it's just nothing compared with being there. When you look at the sun rising over the icy flutings of a peak, or stand on a really airy ridge with a huge amount of exposure and jagged

peaks all around, it's a thrill. The sheer architecture of mountains is spectacular.

I suppose the other exciting aspect of it is the adventure:
the challenge of finding a safe way through to wherever you
want to go—usually the summit. It's really a case of breaking
it down into manageable sections. Because you have to take so
many factors into consideration, it becomes a totally absorbing intellectual challenge. I've never played chess, but it
seems so dull compared to the option of going out on a
mountain and being able to exercise your mind in that same
way. The planning involved, foreseeing problems which might
eventuate if you take a certain path . . . all that makes it very
complex. And what makes it even more exciting is the serious penalty for being wrong—maybe the ultimate penalty.

Perhaps the closest I've come to paying that ultimate price
was when a recalcitrant piton I was removing from the
summit of Gasherbrum IV caused me to lose my balance and
fall down the 3000-metre west face. I was roped to my partner and miraculously he managed to arrest my fall after 20
metres. I was totally winded and for a few anxious moments
was unable to do anything as I dangled on the end of the rope,
my dead weight pulling my partner from his ledge. Luckily,
when I got my breath back—or what little of it was available
at 8000 metres—I was able to find some holds, take my
weight off the rope and eventually climb back up from the
brink of oblivion. While I certainly hope never to have that
sort of experience again, the possibility that something like it
could happen keeps you alert. That danger is one of the elements which makes climbing so exhilarating; another is the
satisfaction of the urge to explore the world in a physical

sense. Mountains provide some of the last vestiges of opportunity to do that.

There is also inner space to conquer. When people go on treks through the foothills of Nepal, or wherever, it is often a seminal experience. They start to find that their direction in life has changed and that their priorities might not be the same as they were before they left. I think it's healthy to continue to strive. To be wholly content with one's life is to stagnate because it's no longer a situation where you are learning, and one of the exciting things in life is to keep growing. In terms of travel, I would never go and look at a town of the future. I'm far more fascinated by where we came from because that's where I can learn about myself. I think the greatest mistake we can make is to ignore the past because it is only by understanding our past that we can arm ourselves with what's necessary to progress.

Nepal only opened up to the outside world in the 1950s, so before then it was very isolated. It didn't even have a road into it from the outside, and most of the places where one goes trekking in Nepal are still several days' walk from a road or, particularly, an airport. I suppose that is one of the reasons I go back to Nepal so often. The people tend to be representations of an earlier type of human being; they are more natural, with a wonderful enthusiasm and spontaneity. In my experience, the more remote the village people, the more fascinating they are. What makes them interesting is not just their lifestyle but their character.

It's almost as if their innocence is complemented by a more civilised mentality because they derive from cultures which developed very early in human history. They have the discipline of civility which tends to be a very sobering influence on human nature but perhaps their isolation has tempered that aspect, making it regress in favour of a more childlike *joie de vivre*. By necessity of their situation, they have to look after each other and you can see that concern for others in their hospitality to travellers. They're generally very welcoming and take an interest in your well-being—in fact, they'd do anything to help. Where else in the world could a dozen grubby foreigners turn up unannounced to camp in someone's yard, or even their family room, and be welcomed with genuine delight and then be plied senseless with the best alcohol in town?

This naturalness of the hill people is very attractive and it's one reason why Nepal and other parts of the Himalaya are so popular and so different to the Alps or the Andes.

When you go with a group of people into mountains, you step out of the normal world and the isolation draws you together. You get to know people so much better because, I suppose, you discover a commonality. Everyone can appreciate spectacular sunsets or a fierce blizzard, and it's that shared experience which bonds you. I think, too, in some primitive sense, it reminds you of the warmth of being in intimate contact with a small group of people. Often the saddest part of a trip is the end when your little group ceases to share the trials and triumphs of the journey; the constituents are scattered in all directions into the cold and fragmented world of 'normal' life. You have become dependent upon one another because for that period of time you have been travelling through life together.

Everything is more accentuated in a mountain environment and it can be exasperating. Many times I have cursed myself for taking a particular route, or doing a particular trip and I think to myself, 'What the hell am I doing this for?' But challenge is one of the great things about travel. I hate organised tours where you are not tested in any way. I'm happy to be pushed by natural elements or a situation precipitated by, say, the onset of bad weather. Better to be pushed in that way than by human cause—like a plane strike, a fire in a hotel. It is actually the hard parts of a trek or a drive which, in retrospect, are the best. If you have just been through a really bad blizzard or survived a fairly traumatic situation, then your perception of your surroundings is heightened. You feel more alive.

Humans attach a tremendous amount of symbolism to mountains because of their loftiness. I've always viewed the physical act of climbing a mountain as symbolic of the human journey, of striving to do better, grappling to understand the world we live in, and aspiring to improve our situation. For me, mountains represent all that struggle. I suppose mountain climbing could be described as a futile act, because it's very hard work and in the case of climbing at high altitude in alpine situations, it's downright dangerous. Nevertheless, in spite of its apparent uselessness, conquering a mountain is very fulfilling.

Mountains are also tremendously rich places to learn about personal responsibility for yourself and your own actions. Eventually, with experience, you can plan your own trips and, if you like, take over the whole management of an expedition, and that gives you self-confidence. It is a tremendously liberating experience to discover confidence. Everybody has it: it just depends how deeply it's buried.

Perhaps the greatest thing of all about mountains is their therapeutic ability to regenerate your soul. **99**

Dances with whales

MIMI MACPHERSON
Tour operator

"The first contact I had with a whale was to hear its haunting song over an underwater microphone—a hydrophone—in Hervey Bay, Queensland. The moment reduced me to tears and, in a way, changed my life.

I have always lived near the ocean—it's been a life-long love. Our family holidays were spent at the seaside and, as children, my sister Elle and brother Ben and I spent long, lazy summers sailing, swimming and water-skiing or paddling about among the rocks, looking for oysters.

So I suppose it's hardly surprising that I chose to follow a career that would keep me near the water. Whales, however, were not part of the master plan; that connection just happened. In the late '80s, I was lucky enough to be offered a job aboard a large sailing boat venture operating in Sydney Harbour. Fantastic, I thought, with derring-do visions of myself hurling out the spinnaker, tying up quay-side and pulling up the sails in fast and furious Sydney-to-Hobart racing fashion.

Life at sea, however, was not to be that romantic. It meant cleaning toilets, peeling potatoes and serving behind the bar. But I was out on the ocean every day, which was all that really mattered. I worked hard and soon found myself assuming a major role in the operation of the company's administration and sales. In 1989, the boat headed north to Hervey Bay to operate whale-watching tours. I went along for the ride but was rather sceptical about the whole venture.

I knew absolutely nothing about these enormous mammals and, as they were endangered, I thought the chances of spotting one would be very slim indeed. Even after we arrived at Hervey Bay, I remained far from optimistic.

Several exploratory cruises were planned before we lowered the gangplank for business. Our first reconnaissance was made in a small dinghy—we had heard there were whales there but the bay was very big and the boat small so we saw nothing. In a last ditch to locate whales, we decided to lower the hydrophone. We heard plenty: the bay was full of their song. It was simply awesome. I was hooked and have been taking people out onto the bay to view whales ever since. Whale-watching has become enormously popular in the Hervey Bay region and there are now 19 companies operating in season. That may sound like a lot but even with that number, it doesn't detract from the experience.

The great thing about whale-watching is that it's on their terms: the bay is the whales' backyard and you, as a visitor, must behave as any polite guest should. No more than three boats may pass within 300 metres of a whale at any one time. That's not to say there's no close contact: the whales frequently approach vessels of their own volition and this can lead to the most extraordinary moments.

Some two years after arriving at Hervey Bay, I was out on the water when two whales approached. They were messing about, swimming in circles and being very amorous, hugging each other with their pectoral fins—which, incidentally, are very similar to the human arm in terms of bone structure. I reached my hand down into the water and one of the whales rolled onto its side to look at me. It then lifted its head straight up and touched my hand. I'm sure it was a deliberate action on the whale's part, an attempt to make contact.

Every such contact is extremely emotional and there are few people who remain unmoved even by a glimpse of a whale—many of our passengers are reduced to tears. I've seen a deaf woman hear whale song through the hull of the boat. There's always the passenger who expects a sideshow but that's not what the exercise is all about. It's simply to do with observing whales doing normal whale things in their natural environment.

There is something about whales which strikes a chord in most people. They are mysterious, awe-inspiringly big—one whale can weigh as much as 600 people—yet gentle and intelligent. What other wild animal actually comes up to greet you?

And there is probably nowhere better in the world to commune with these wonderful creatures than Hervey Bay. The bay is also home to hundreds and hundreds of dolphins and sea turtles as well as minke and humpback whales; it also used to have one of the world's largest dugong populations. It's very accessible, too: Hervey Bay airport is a 35-minute flight from Brisbane or about two hours' drive north of Noosa. Hervey Bay is also the gateway to Fraser Island, the world's largest sand isle, and it has the most temperate climate in Australia. In fact, it's paradise!

The whales use Hervey Bay as a resting place—like a lovely warm bath where they can flop for a few days during their migration between July and October each year. Sometimes they spend up to two weeks and there are generally up to 60 whales in the bay at any one time and around 600 during the course of the season.

It's quite another story on Maui. This Hawaiian island is one of the world's principal whale-watching centres but the water is deeper and colder and the whales tend to be more aggressive. They're not terribly inquisitive and generally don't show a great deal of interest in the tourist boats.

We're very lucky to have such wonderful conditions for observing whales in Australia. During winter, they travel some 5000 kilometres from the cold waters of Antarctica to warmer climates off Australia's east and west coasts and the Pacific islands to mate and give birth.

The calves are born minus a protective layer of fat but rectify that situation very quickly by drinking up to 600 litres of milk a day—this milk has the consistency of yoghurt and a fat content five times greater than human breast milk. The calf gains around 20 to 30 kilos a day; the adult whales, however, barely eat for their 10,000-kilometre round journey.

They are thought to give birth a little north of Hervey Bay in a mysterious location which is yet to be discovered. We've observed a couple of births in the bay but we're sure they were accidents—a sort of 'giving birth in the cab on the way to the hospital' scenario.

It seems that the same whales return to the bay year after year, and some are instantly recognisable. Mad Maxine, for example, has a badly damaged dorsal fin and looks like a razorback. We began by calling her Mad Max until we realised she was a female. The marine biologists, however, recognise many of the whales as they spend hours and hours studying their photographs and tracking their progress around the Pacific.

We have all become very attached to 'our' whales and I couldn't imagine not seeing them every season. I'm not alone in feeling this way. We have visitors who return again and again to see the whales: one family comes to Hervey Bay every year and they take five or six cruises each time.

Hervey Bay and its whales are obviously deeply entrenched in my heart, and, while I have many other favourite beach haunts around the world, I find it hard to travel far beyond the east coast of Australia. Every year, I drive the coast between Sydney and Hervey Bay stopping at Forster, which has incredible beaches and wonderful oysters, Byron Bay where I never tire of all those great little restaurants, and Southport on the Gold Coast. A lot of people find Surfers Paradise tacky but I don't—the beach is beautiful and the water's clean and warm. I stay at the Sheraton Mirage, which is my favourite, favourite resort, surrounded by wonderful swimming pools. I take a room on the ground floor and every morning, I charge straight onto the beach for a brisk run and vigorous workout. Then it's off to the restaurant to gorge on a huge breakfast—and undo all my good work.

I also adore the Four Seasons Resort on Maui where, unbelievably, you can watch the whales breaching just offshore while lounging in the resort pool and hear them singing while snorkelling.

Another favourite retreat is Lake McKenzie on Fraser Island. It's a beautiful freshwater lake surrounded by rainforest and white sand. The water is so pure that it instantly softens your hair. I once camped by the lake for three days; at night I lay attempting to count the stars in the sky and listening to the small animals scuttling about in the undergrowth.

I find it sad that too few people have discovered this kind of holiday. Visiting a crowded, bustling city for a spot of shopping isn't my idea of fun. The best kind of travel is where you get to relax, preferably by the water, and revel in absolute peace and quiet. **"**

Making
tracks

TONY WHEELER
Publisher and Writer

"Walking is highly necessary for a travel writer. I think it is the only way to really find things when you travel. I've made myself a promise to try and do a long walk each year. It's something you really can't hurry— everything else you do, you can do too fast. But when you're walking, you simply can't rush it, you can only go at the pace that God intended and it's rather nice that you see the world no faster than your feet allow you to.

I remember when I was nine or ten years old, being fascinated by maps and mapping things. I'd go off on all-day walks on the weekend, travelling along the coastline close to where my parents lived at Highcliffe, near Bournemouth on the south coast of England, mapping things as I went. I suppose I was an enthusiastic explorer from an early age.

Now, when we are doing a new Lonely Planet book, I always begin by preparing a map or, when updating a book, I start by revising the map, and the only way you can do that properly is by walking. If it's a new book, I place things on the map first and later I think about what's going to be written about the sights, the attractions, the restaurants, hotels and so on.

I am not a rabid walker who walks non-stop all day and whose life revolves around it. I just like to walk if I have the time and the excuse to do it. Every country has different elements which make walking interesting. In Nepal, for example, the terrain roller-coasters up and down so steeply that how long a walk takes bears no relationship to the distance. On the other hand, walking in Britain, you know you're going to cover about two and a half miles an hour, so if you have a twenty-five-mile walk it's going to take you ten hours. Add an hour or so for lunch and you've got a twelve-hour day coming up.

Walking certainly doesn't have to be uncomfortable. In Nepal it may take a lot of physical effort but it's no great hardship if you do walk in the traditional manner with Sherpas, guides, porters and a cup of tea in the tent first thing in the morning.

Walking in Britain is quite the opposite, in that you do everything yourself. There are no porters to carry your pack or Sherpa guides to make sure you don't miss the tricky forks in the track, but even without a whole team to put your tent up and roll out your sleeping bag, you're still very comfortable. On British long-distance walks you often find a pub at lunchtime and another one to have a beer with your evening meal, and you generally stay each night in bed and breakfast places.

Nepal, apart from the limited number of places where there are roads, is connected by footpaths. In England, very often the walking tracks relate back to medieval trade routes or Roman roads. As you come into a village, you know there's a main road that runs through it carrying the traffic, but the one you take into the village is probably the route that was there a thousand years ago. In Nepal the walking route is still the main route, and the way you arrive in the village is exactly the same as you would have a thousand years ago. I find that sort of medieval aspect to the country fascinating.

At bookshop talks, I am often asked to nominate my favourite country but I find such specifics very limiting. As far as the best walks are concerned, Nepal has to be the place because it is so spectacular with its big scenery and fantastic views. It's an old line, but a lot of people go to Nepal simply to see the mountains and the scenery, but when they come back it's the Nepalese people, not the Himalayan peaks, which they will remember. They are such friendly and outgoing people, but when it comes to running treks they do it very thoroughly and professionally. After all, they've been escorting mountaineering trips to the Himalaya for a century.

One of the best walks I've done, and one which went extremely smoothly, was in Nepal with a group of children. My wife, Maureen, and I took our two, Tashi and Kieran, and some friends came along with theirs as well. It was the Nepalese school holidays and the cook brought his two sons and another Nepalese trek operator sent his 12-year-old daughter. We ended up with equal numbers of Nepalese and Australian kids: there were certainly more kids than adults!

We chose the Helambu Circuit—a circular walk which takes about eight days and stays below four thousand metres. A circuit walk is always nice because you get back to where you started, and this one was just the right length. Three or four days is too short and, with kids, two weeks is too long. All the kids really enjoyed it, they got on like a house on fire. Every night, we'd get into camp and they'd be running around like crazy. It was amazing, they weren't tired at all—we were worn out, though! I was pretty impressed with the youngest, two six-year-olds, who both walked for the whole eight days.

Maureen and I had taken our kids walking in Nepal before but the others had never really travelled in the Third World so it was quite an experience for them. They all wanted to go back and do it again.

In 1996, Kieran and I walked the circuit of Mont Blanc with three other children and four other adults. What I liked about it was the idea of walking from country to country, as the circuit takes you through Switzerland, France and Italy. It's more British than Australian in style, in that you are generally close to civilisation all the time and you are going from village to village. Quite a bit of it is almost a walk through urban territory—as most of Western Europe is these days. It's also seasonal, and the best time is the northern spring or early autumn. In summer, it's too crowded and during winter it's closed.

The French have this reputation for being unfriendly but we met some amazingly helpful people and had some surprisingly pleasant episodes in France doing that circuit. The first night on the track we'd just arrived from Australia, everyone was jetlagged, there were a couple of young kids and the place we intended to stay at that night had closed for the season. By this time it was getting rather late, we were stumbling around in the dark and, by the time we got to the next village, reassuringly called Le Planet, and found a place to stay, we were all very hungry and everything was shut.

We managed to phone a taxi service in the next village down the valley. They came and picked us up and drove us to Argentiére, and half an hour later we were enjoying steak, pommes frites and red wine. By the time we paid the bill, the kids were falling asleep and we asked if we could phone for a taxi. The patron wouldn't hear of it, he told us he had a car, the chef had a car, and they would drive us back to our village. Now you'd hardly expect that sort of thing to happen anywhere . . . but in France!

The following day, I was the first one up and decided to walk the three kilometres to the next village. I found a supermarket, bought food for breakfast and was walking back, carrying armfuls of baguettes, when this woman pulled up in her car and asked if she could give me a ride. Again this seemed delightfully unFrench, picking up a hitchhiker who wasn't even hitchhiking!

The Mont Blanc circuit is a great walk. We had superb weather, the views are amazing and we saw it from both sides. However, at one point we had to abandon the walk because we couldn't find accommodation. We retreated to Chamonix and took the amazing cable car ride over the top of the Mont Blanc massif and down into Italy, where we resumed the walk on the Italian side of the border, missing two days of the circuit. That was a disappointment, although the cable car views just about compensated.

I've been through all the extremes of walking—with the whole family, with a bunch of friends, just Maureen and I, or even solo, but rarely do you walk on your own. For example, we are doing a walking guide to Britain and I covered the Pennine Way recently, walking by myself. At first, you may be with someone for a day or two, and then they may take a day's rest or drop back, but you catch up with someone else or somebody overtakes you and, toward the end, you start to form a group. At night, we'd all meet in the pub, and over the last few days it felt like something from *Canterbury Tales*, everyone homing in on 'Canterbury' as we got to be a bigger and bigger group.

For some reason, the Pennine Way attracts a lot of crazy characters, perhaps because it has a reputation for being Britain's toughest walk. It's a long walk, more than four hundred kilometres, so it takes most people two or more weeks. It starts in the Peak District in the north midlands and follows the central spine of England all the way north to the Scottish border. Then it follows the border for a while before finally popping across to finish in Scotland. It's not just the distance which accounts for its tough reputation, however. Teetering along the top of England you're buffeted by every gale-force wind making its way from the North Sea to the Irish Sea, or vice versa. And if British weather isn't bad enough, the Pennine Way is also famously boggy. At every pub along the way walkers would gather to recount horrible tales of being stuck in mud up to their knees, their thighs, their waists, their necks . . . or even further.

Global warming apart, they aren't going to be able to do much about British weather, but in recent years there has been an enormous amount of track improvements, and as a result the boggy stretches are mainly a thing of the past. Stone-slabbed paths wind across some of the most infamous bogs, which has not only made the walking much easier, it's made navigation much simpler. No longer can walkers whinge about how they were hopelessly lost for days on end while inextricably stuck in the mud. Plus, I had excellent weather for most of the walk, so for me at least it wasn't 'tough' at all. Nevertheless, the Pennine Way still attracts the characters. I met one person who had done it eleven times— if you take two and a half weeks and multiply that by eleven times, it's a pretty large chunk out of your life!

I also did the walk along Hadrian's Wall, which goes from coast to coast, following the old Roman wall which separated England, and civilisation, from Scotland, and the barbarians, but that was a bit disappointing—bits of it are very good but quite a lot goes through industrial areas and often there is no trace of the wall. The walking authorities in Britain are trying to turn it into a proper walk, avoiding the dull industrial areas.

Another very pleasant British walk I did was the Cotswold Way, which is an extremely civilised route. It winds through the Cotswolds, starting just south of Stratford-upon-Avon and ending at Bath. This is a walk you can do in real luxury, you can even stay in fancy hotels and eat at Michelin-starred restaurants on a couple of nights. The first day's walk takes you to a pretty little village called Broadway where the Lygon Arms Hotel has a reputation for being one of Britain's best country hotels. If you can afford it, it's rather nice turning up there hot and sweaty, and slinging your backpack over to the doorman to carry to your room. If you decide walking is too much like hard work, you could call for a chopper evacuation the next morning—the hotel has a helicopter landing pad!

Of course, walking doesn't have to be about long treks. Last year we were working on a guide to French Polynesia and I found that Tahiti and the other islands have some wonderful shorter walks. It's real struggle-through-the-jungle stuff, but you get to places where there are just fantastic views, from the top of cliffs which drop right down to the sea. On the island of Moorea, in particular, a couple of walks are along ancient trails that lead from village to village. The walk—'struggle' might be a better definition—up to the knife-like ridge called the Three Coconut Trees Pass is a particular knockout, although when you get to the top there's only one coconut tree. The other two blew down in a cyclone.

I did a little bit of walking in Japan about five years ago, which was very interesting. The one I remember best was climbing Mt Fuji to see the dawn. This is a real Japanese mass-tourism experience. At the height of summer, there can be around two thousand people climbing to the top each night! You can actually climb Fuji any time of year, although a mid-winter ascent is strictly for the real mountaineers. Like many things in Japan, however, there is a best time to do it, and that official climbing 'season' in July and August is the most crowded.

I started off too early, which meant hanging around at the top. The last bus to the starting point arrives at 10 pm and you walk all night to get there at dawn, the coldest hour of the day. The views were fantastic but it was very, very cold. It was also a very, very Japanese experience.

The other Japanese walk which I really enjoyed was the ascent of Mt Ishizuchi-san, the highest mountain in Shikoku, in fact the highest mountain in all of western Japan. You start off with a cable car ride followed by a climb or a chairlift ride, then it's down through one forest, up through another, and finally a steep clamber up a rock face to the summit. You can take steps up this final stretch but it's more fun to follow the official pilgrimage route—this is a holy mountain—and clamber up the rock face using the *kusari*, heavy chains draped down the face.

The summit is a popular local destination but it's not the sort of place where foreigners usually go, and there was a bunch of Japanese at the top who thought I was a most curious sight. My Japanese was virtually non-existent but despite no common language, they were so friendly. It's been my experience in Japan that if you're in a place where it is unusual to see foreigners, the Japanese will go out of their way to help you. They are great walkers and you meet a lot of them in Nepal.

There are a lot of longer walks in Japan that I would love to do—in fact there are lots of walks in many countries I'd like to try. I actually made a list of those I must get around to doing—I've never done any of the great walks in New Zealand, for example, and there's a desert walk to the west of Alice Springs that follows the MacDonnell Ranges, and one day I must do the Inca Trail in South America, a week-long walk which ends at Machu Picchu.

The circuit of Mt Kailash in Tibet is one that I'd especially like to do. It's about sixty kilometres around the base of the mountain. Mt Kailash is just north of the Tibet border with Nepal, and a place of great religious significance as it's the birthplace of Lord Shiva. The Ganges, Indus and Brahma rivers all have their sources there so it is a major pilgrimage site for a number of religions. However, it's an area that the Chinese are very sensitive about, quite apart from being very remote. Simply getting there is a difficult operation, tough travel for five or six days on bad roads at high altitudes.

The real thing with walks is that they're very much about how it goes at the time, who you're with, the conversations you have, what the weather is like. Often, it is not so much the place itself but the experience of how and what got you there that remains in your mind and in your heart.

I remember a story told to me by Stan Armington, who wrote our *Trekking in the Nepal Himalaya* guide. One day, he was sitting in a Nepalese valley, looking across at a walking trail on the other side, and the Sherpa he was with said you could tell the nationality of walkers from miles away.

'Look,' the Sherpa said, 'walkers in neat, evenly spaced, single file. Japanese.

'Now another group, again in regimented order, but all walking with ski poles. Germans.

'Now here comes somebody all alone. Then after ten minutes, a group of three or four. Ten minutes later, somebody else alone. Five minutes pass and another cluster of walkers. Australians.'

I really like this idea that there's a style of walking which different nationalities acquire. **"**

Biographical notes
on interviewees

STEPHANIE ALEXANDER trained as a librarian and teacher before entering the restaurant business, opening Jamaica House in Melbourne with her first husband. Her work and writing have influenced the evolution of eating in Australia, and her restaurant, Stephanie's, is regarded as one of the best in the country. Her encyclopaedic fifth book, *Cook's Companion*, has been an unqualified success, as has her latest, Stephanie Alexander and Maggie Beer's *Tuscan Cookbook*. Stephanie is also the creative force behind Richmond Hill Café and Larder, a new retail outlet in Melbourne.

GLENN A. BAKER is a writer and broadcaster specialising in music, the arts and travel. He is the author of 13 books—the most recent being *Faces, Places and Barely Human Races*—and has contributed articles to more than 200 publications. In the 1980s, Glenn was a three-time recipient of the BBC's 'Rock Brain of the Universe' title, and in 1995 he won the inaugural Air New Zealand travel writing award. He is regularly seen on Channel 9's *Good Morning Australia*. Glenn lives in Sydney with his wife and six children.

GRAEME BLUNDELL is an actor, writer and director. He helped co-found the Pram Factory Theatre in Melbourne in 1970, and achieved national recognition when he starred in the film *Alvin Purple*. He went on to be taken seriously in countless plays, films and television series. Besides writing articles for magazines and newspapers—especially reviews of his favourite reading: crime novels and true crime books—Graeme has compiled a book of anecdotes about the history of Australian theatre, has co-written a biography of Brett Whiteley and is completing a biography of Graham Kennedy.

TIM BOWDEN is a Sydney broadcaster, radio and TV documentary-maker, oral historian and author. He hosted the ABC-TV listener and viewer reaction program *Backchat* from 1986 to June 1994. A former foreign correspondent and current affairs reporter and producer for the ABC, his published books are: *Changi Photographer—George Aspinall's Record of Captivity*; *One Crowded Hour—Neil Davis, Combat Cameraman*; *The Way My Father Tells It—The Story of an Australian Life*; *Antarctica and Back in Sixty Days*; and *The Silence Calling—Australians in Antarctica 1947-97*. For the past 10 years, Tim Bowden has been actively broadcasting, writing and researching Australian activities in Antarctica. He received an Order of Australia for services to public broadcasting in June 1994. In May 1997 he was awarded an honorary degree of Doctor of Letters from the University of Tasmania.

SARINA BRATTON embarked on a successful career in tourism after injury cut short an outstanding sporting career, which included simultaneous Australian medals in three sports: gymnastics, diving and trampolining. She has twice been a finalist for the Businesswoman of the Year Award and was the 1995 winner of the Avon Spirit of Achievement Business Award. Sarina has held senior board positions with the NSW State Transit Authority, the Australian Maritime Safety Authority and the Sydney Paralympic Organising Committee. Until recently, she was Vice President and General Manager Asia-Pacific for Cunard Line and is now Managing Director of Norwegian Capricorn Line, a new Sydney-based cruising company.

MARELE DAY has travelled extensively and lived in Italy, France and Ireland. An award-winning author, she is one of Australia's top crime writers. Her Claudia Valentine novels— *The Life and Crimes of Harry Lavender*, *The Case of the Chinese Boxes*, *The Last Tango of Dolores Delgado* and *The Disappearances of Madalena Grimaldi*—have been successfully published in Britain, the USA and Germany. Her latest book is a literary novel, *Lambs of God*. She lives in Sydney, by the harbour.

BARRY DICKINS is one of Australia's best-loved playwrights. Born on Melbourne Cup Day, 1949, he says he turned into a poet simultaneously because his mother, Edna, kept laughing through the delivery. Barry has been a hedge-trimmer, librettist, librarian, love poet and English teacher. His first performed play was *The Rotten Teeth Show*, presented at the now-not-there Pram Factory Theatre in Carlton. The moral of the comedy was, 'You cannot defend yourself without teeth' and one evening it played to 200 unemployed dentists. Aside from regularly contributing to major Australian newspapers, Barry declares, 'I enjoy myself for a living.'

PAUL DYER is one of Australia's leading specialists in period performing styles. Paul founded the Australian Brandenburg Orchestra in 1990 as a natural outcome of his long experience as a performer and teacher of baroque and classical music. He studied piano and harpsichord at the Sydney Conservatorium and graduated with B. Mus., B. Mus. Ed. and ATCL (perf.), then studied with Bob van Asperen at the Royal Conservatory in The Hague, obtaining a postgraduate diploma in early music. In Australia he has a busy career as a harpsichord soloist and continuo player, with regular engagements with the Sydney and Queensland Symphony Orchestras, Australia Ensemble, Australian Chamber Orchestra and Opera Australia. Paul has conducted the Sydney Symphony Orchestra, the Australian Youth Orchestra and the Queensland Philharmonic Orchestra. An inspiring teacher, he has been in demand as an instructor in harpsichord and performance practice at leading music schools in Australia. In 1995 Paul was awarded a Churchill Fellowship to undertake advanced studies in baroque performance in France, England, Italy, Belgium and the Netherlands.

DAIZY GEDEON is a journalist and filmmaker who has worked in Australia, Britain, the Middle East and the USA. Her documentary, *Lebanon . . . Imprisoned Splendour,* co-presented by Omar Sharif, was awarded the Silver Screen Award at the 1996 US International Film and Video Festival where it was selected from among 1500 entries from 35 countries. It was also screened at the invitation-only Boston Film Festival in 1996, where it was voted Best of the Shorts. The film also received a High Commendation from the Human Rights and

Equal Opportunity Commission. Daizy is now involved in filmmaking on a permanent basis.

CHRISTINE GEE co-founded Australian Himalayan Expeditions in Canberra in 1975, a company which was to become an international leader in adventure travel, chalking up such world firsts as trekking to Everest via Tibet, cycling programs in China, rafting in Tibet, and trekking in Outer Mongolia and the former Soviet Union. In 1987, Christine was appointed as the Honorary Royal Nepalese Consul-General for NSW and she is actively involved in raising funds for community-based projects in Nepal. Christine also runs a successful marketing and promotions company and acts as publicist to author Bryce Courtenay and other high-profile media clients.

MARION HALLIGAN was born in Newcastle, NSW, and grew up by the sea. She now lives in Canberra, and spends time in France whenever she can. Her 11 books include the novels *Spider Cup*, *Lovers' Knots* and *Wishbone*. *Eat My Words* and *Cockles of the Heart* are books of autobiography, travel and food, along with *Those Women who go to Hotels*, co-authored with Lucy Frost. *Out of the Picture* is based on photographs in the National Library; her *Collected Stories* was published to wide acclaim in 1997. Prizes include the Steele Rudd Award, the Braille Book of the Year, the *Age* Book of the Year, the ACT Book of the Year, the Nita B. Kibble Award and the Geraldine Pascall Prize.

JANE HOLMES is a Melbourne-based journalist, radio and TV personality. From 1993 to 1996 she was an on-camera presenter for Channel 7's successful show *Talk to the Animals*, filing reports on all creatures great and small, from locations as diverse and exotic as Antarctica, Chile, the United States, the UK, India, Asia and, of course, Africa.

SUSAN KUROSAWA is the award-winning Travel Editor of *The Australian* and a columnist for *The Australian Magazine*. She began travelling at the age of three when she boarded the *Arcadia* with her mother to join her foreign correspondent father for a life abroad. She has lived and worked in Japan and Hong Kong and has been widely published in Australian newspapers, magazines and anthologies. *Places in the Heart* is her fourth book. Susan also travels on behalf of AUSTCARE to raise public awareness of the plight of refugees in war-affected countries.

KATE LLEWELLYN was born at Tumby Bay, South Australia. After many years in the Blue Mountains west of Sydney, she has recently moved to the south coast of NSW. She has published six books of poetry and her first major prose writing, *The Waterlily*, was published in 1987 to wide acclaim, followed by her successful Blue Mountains trilogy. Kate Llewellyn is also known for her travel writing and has published three books which resonate with the sights, sounds and smells of exotic places.

TIM MACARTNEY-SNAPE, AM, OAM, spent the first 12 years of his life in Tanzania, where he was born to an Australian father and British mother. Best known as the first person ever to climb the whole of Mt Everest's 8874 metres, Tim gained the summit on May 11, 1990. This achievement followed 12 years of successful Himalayan ascents on 10 major expeditions, all of them undertaken without bottled oxygen in a lightweight style. A trained biologist with a BSc from ANU, Tim is also a qualified outdoor instructor, author of three books and a popular inspirational speaker. He is chairman of the Nepal Eye Program Australia and a director of the foundation for Humanities Adulthood, an organisation with a philosophical and biological basis interested in the long-term wellbeing of humanity. When not travelling, Tim lives 100 kilometres south-πwest of Sydney with his partner, Stacy Rodger.

MIMI MACPHERSON runs Mimi Macpherson Whale Watch Expeditions, an award-winning tourism operation based at Hervey Bay, to the north of Queensland's Sunshine Coast. Her company is a major sponsor of the Pacific Whale Foundation and a supporter of many other environmental conservation bodies. She travels the world to promote and market Queensland's Hervey Bay as a prime whale-watching destination.

JOHN AND ROS MORIARTY are the proprietors of Balarinji Design, a company with a team of Aboriginal and non-Aboriginal artists who blend the indigenous art of Australia with contemporary graphics and distinctive landscape colours. Balarinji markets its fashion label in retail stores in Australia, Japan, France, Italy, the Caribbean and Canada. Among Balarinji's many prestigious design commissions have been two Qantas 747 aircraft—Wunala Dreaming and Nalanji Dreaming—and Balarinji is featured in the collections of Sydney's Powerhouse Museum, the National Gallery in

Canberra and the Flinders University Art Museum in Adelaide. The Moriartys now live in Sydney but maintain strong links with Adelaide and their special retreat in the South Australian Coorong.

RICHARD NEVILLE came to prominence in the sixties when he launched *Oz* magazine in Sydney and London, and has remained a controversial social commentator ever since. The author of five books, including *Hippie Hippie Shake* and *Out of My Mind*, Neville is co-founder of Australia's first Futurists' Foundation. He lives in the Blue Mountains, west of Sydney.

STEVE PARISH is one of Australia's best-known photographers of the natural environment. His love of the sea began when he was nine, while spearfishing in his native South Australia. At age 16 he was handed an underwater camera and took his first shot. When it was projected onto a screen at a reunion, everyone clapped, and in that instant Parish discovered two loves: an audience and photography. He joined the navy at age 18 and in the ensuing 10 years he continued to study fish and photograph marine life. In 1975 he joined Queensland National Parks, and then came five years as a consultant to publishers before starting his own Brisbane-based enterprise, Steve Parish Publishing, in 1985. He runs this company with his wife and partner, Jan; they employ 95 people in the creation and distribution of a wide range of books, posters, calendars, cards and other products featuring Australian landscapes and wildlife.

BILL PEACH became one of the best-known faces on Australian TV when he presented the ABC's *This Day Tonight* for eight years. He has made many documentary programs about Australia and has presented successful promotional campaigns for the Australian Tourist Commission. Bill has written 10 books on Australian history and travel and leads groups on aerial tours with Aircruising Australia, the company which pioneered luxury air travel to the Outback. Bill has been made a Member of the Order of Australia (AM) for his contributions to the media and tourism.

MARY ROSSI graduated from Sydney University in 1944 with Honours in English Literature and History. Before her marriage to Sydney businessman Theo Rossi, she worked as a political and legal researcher, speechwriter and librarian. In the 1950s and early 1960s, Mary was a compere of women's programs for ABC-TV. In 1970, she formed Mary Rossi Travel in Sydney, a successful agency which has been presented with many awards for excellence. In 1975, Mary Rossi was named NSW's Mother of the Year; in 1976, she was awarded the Queen's Jubilee Medal, and in 1979 the Order of the British Empire (OBE). Widely recognised as the doyenne of the Australian travel industry, Mary has 10 children and 25 grandchildren.

HARRY SEIDLER has received more than 40 awards for his work from the Royal Australian Institute of Architects, including five Sulman Medals and the Gold Medal of the Institute in 1976. He was awarded an OBE in 1972 and the Order of Australia (AC) in 1987. In 1996, Harry was awarded the Royal Gold Medal by the Royal Institute of British Architects and, in the same year, the Austrian Cross of Honour (First Class) for Art and Science. His work is built upon and extends the tenets of modern architecture, with many completed projects in Australia, Europe, Central America and Asia, including the Australian Embassy in Paris. He is presently working on a self-contained community housing project for 2500 people on the banks of the Danube, in his native Vienna.

CHARMAINE SOLOMON is the author of 29 cookbooks, including *The Complete Asian Cookbook*, which sells worldwide in four languages. On TV and video, through her writing and at cooking schools, she has taught people how to capture the essence of Asian food. Her latest appearance outside Australia was at the International Association of Culinary Professionals conference in New Orleans, where her topic was the Asian influence on Australian cuisine. Charmaine Solomon lives with her family in Sydney.

VINCE SORRENTI is one of Australia's favourite comedians. As a student of architecture at Sydney University, Vince made his name as a comic working at the Sydney Comedy Store and was a nationally known performer before he graduated in 1985. Vince has performed around the world, averaging almost 200 appearances a year over the past decade, and has appeared on TV shows as diverse as *Hey, Hey, It's Saturday*, *Burke's Backyard*, *Neighbours* and *The Eric Bana Show*. Vince is also a popular corporate speaker and master of ceremonies. He is presently writing a novel.

PRIA VISWALINGAM was born in Kota Bharu, Kelantan, Malaysia. He moved to Kuala Lumpur as a child and lived there until 1975, leaving Malaysia to continue school in England. He spent two years in London before moving to

Singapore in 1977 and then to Perth, Western Australia, in 1978. He worked as a radio reporter there, then moved to SBS television in 1989. At SBS he has continued to produce and present international travel documentaries. *A Fork in the Road* is now in its fourth consecutive series. Pria is married with twins and lives in Sydney.

TETSUYA WAKUDA is one of Sydney's most celebrated chefs. He arrived in Australia from Japan in 1982 and opened Tetsuya's restaurant in Rozelle in 1989. Since 1992, Tetsuya's has been awarded three chef's hats in the *Sydney Morning Herald Good Food Guide*, and in 1993 and 1996 was named the Remy/*Gourmet Traveller* Restaurant of the Year. Also in 1996, Tetsuya's was named winner of the Diners Club Restaurateurs' Choice Award, and in 1997 it was inducted into the Restaurant and Catering Industry Hall of Fame. Tetsuya has made Sydney his permanent home.

JEFF WATSON is an English-born broadcaster, author and journalist who migrated to Australia in 1971 and has contributed to a number of top current affairs TV programs. In 1979 he devised the popular TV series *Towards 2000*, and is well known as a presenter for *Beyond 2000* and *Getaway*. He is the author of two books and the producer of several documentaries, including *Spitfire over Australia*. In 1991, Jeff was created a Chevalier of the Order of Merit by the late President Mitterand of France.

TONY WHEELER co-founded Lonely Planet Publications with his wife, Maureen, in 1973 after travelling the hippie trail from London to Australia. From humble beginnings with

Across Asia on the Cheap, produced on a kitchen table, Lonely Planet guide books have become a travel institution. The Melbourne-based company now employs 80 writers and has offices in San Francisco, London and Paris. Tony and Maureen live in Melbourne with their two children, Tashi and Kieran.

MIKE WHITNEY, a former fast bowler for NSW and Australian teams, now hosts TV shows *Who Dares Wins* and *Sydney Weekender*, a Saturday afternoon leisure/lifestyle program on the Seven Network. He has also written two books, *Quick Whit* and *Whitticisms: Confessions of a Left Arm Quick*.

SORREL WILBY is an adventurer, author, photographer and artist who began her travels in 1981 with a four-wheel-drive odyssey around Australia. Her books include *Tibet*, *Across the Top* and *Africa: A Timeless Soul*. In 1986, Sorrel received the *Australian Geographic* Award for excellence in extending the Australian spirit of adventure to remote corners of the world. She was the first Australian woman to be elected as a Fellow of the internationally renowned Explorers' Club. She is a reporter on the popular TV travel program, *Getaway*.